# BITTER EDEN

Tatamkhulu Afrika was born in Egypt in 1920 of an Arab father
and a Turkish mother. He was brought to South Africa in 1923,
orphaned and raised by Christian foster parents. He served in
World War II, and was a POW for three years in Italy and
Germany. After the war he has also worked as a barman, a shop
assistant, a bookkeeper and a drummer in a band. He settled in
Cape Town in 1964, when he converted to Islam and joined the
resistance to apartheid. Arrested in 1987 for 'terrorism', he was
listed for five years as a banned person, and he still draws a pension from Umkhonto we Sizwe, the combatant arm of the ANC.
Since 1990, he has published eight volumes of poetry and two
prose works. At the age of seventeen he published an acclaimed
novel in the UK entitled *Broken Earth*, but did not write again
for fifty years. Prizes for poetry include the CNA Début Prize,
two Thomas Pringle Awards, the Olive Schreiner Prize and the
Sanlam Poetry Prize. He presently lives in a little wooden hut in
the back yard of a house in Bo-Kaap, Cape Town.

Praise for *Bitter Eden*:

'How refreshing to hear of the eager acquisition of a début by a man of eighty – a South African, and a poet, to boot. *Bitter Eden* is about ordinary male relationships in extraordinary circumstances'
– Boyd Tonkin, *Independent*

'The admirable independent publisher Arcadia has signed up another overlooked author. *Bitter Eden*, set in a POW camp during the Second World War, is the work of a blind eighty-year-old South African poet and ANC soldier. Wouldn't it be nice if *Bitter Eden* made his fortune?'
– Sam Leith, *Daily Telegraph*

'The highly acclaimed septuagenarian poet has turned his hand to prose and has produced a novel of exceptional quality. It is absorbing and beautifully written. Afrika is still the poet, here in freer form in long and elegant sentences, immaculately constructed, sweeping one along'
– *Mail & Guardian*

'We gain a number of valuable insights into what both participating and non-participating "coloured" people thought and think of Africans and of the struggle' – *Sash*

'A finely crafted début novel that is at once provocative and readable'
– *Femina*

'As a poet Afrika produces gritty, unembroidered verse which captures the lives and moods of people who from circumstance or choice live on the fringes of society. His work is consistently clear, unembroidered, often very moving and has won him South Africa's top literary prizes. This is a well written, finely crafted novel – and a good read'
– *Cape Times*

'Like a steam train, Afrika's story starts sedately, gathers impetus and, without allowing the reader to disembark, becomes an uncontrollable juggernaut hurtling to a disaster bewildering in its implications. Afrika shows with an insider's empathy how, in the myriad battles of our recent past, an even greater number of private wars were lost or won'
– *Argus*

'Had war and fate not intervened, Tatamkhulu Afrika would have been a literary star fifty years ago. Now, aged eighty, he finally makes his début' – *Books* magazine

'So compelling, with the force and immediacy of a strong writer'
– *Weekly Mail & Guardian*

'Compassionate and disturbing' – *The Bookseller*

# BITTER EDEN

## Tatamkhulu Afrika

ARCADIA BOOKS

LONDON

Arcadia Books Ltd
15–16 Nassau Street
London w1w 7ab

First published in Great Britain 2002

A catalogue record for this book is available from the British Library.

isbn 1–900850–70–2

Typeset in Stempel Garamond by Discript, London wc2n 4bn
Printed in the United Kingdom by Bell & Bain Limited, Glasgow

*Arcadia Books distributors are as follows:*

*in the UK and elsewhere in Europe:*
Turnaround Publishers Services
Unit 3, Olympia Trading Estate
Coburg Road
London n22 6tz

*in the USA and Canada:*
Consortium Book Sales and Distribution, Inc.
1045 Westgate Drive
St Paul, MN 55114–1065

*in Australia:*
Tower Books
PO Box 213
Brookvale, NSW 2100

*in New Zealand:*
Addenda
Box 78224
Grey Lynn
Auckland

For Tony and Johan who cared when none else did.

*I* TOUCH THE SCAR ON MY CHEEK and it flinches as though the long-dead tissue had a Lazarus-life of its own.

Uneasily, I stare at the two letters and accompanying neat package which are still where I put them earlier in the day. Within easy reach of my hand, they are a constant and unsettling focus for my mind and eye.

The single envelope in which the letters were posted is also still there. Airmail and drably English in its design, its difference from its local kin both fascinates and disturbs. I am not accustomed any more to receiving mail from abroad.

The one letter, typed under the logo of a firm of lawyers, is a covering letter which starts off by describing how they have only managed to trace me after much trouble and expense, which expense is to be defrayed by the 'deceased's estate'. Then comes the bald statement that it is *he* that has 'passed on' – how I hate that phrase! – after a long illness whose nature they do not disclose and that I have been named in his will as one of the heirs. My legacy, they add, is very small but will no doubt be of some significance to *me* and it is being forwarded under separate cover per registered mail.

The other letter is from him and I knew that straight away. After fifty years of silence, there was still no mistaking the rounded, bold and generously sprawling hand. Closer inspection betrayed the slight shakiness that is beginning to taint my own hand, and I noted this with an unwilling tenderness and a resurgence – as unwilling – of a love that time, it seems, has *too* lightly overlaid.

After reading the letters – but not yet opening the package – I had sat for a long time, staring out of the window and watching gulls and papers whirling up out of the southeaster-ridden street, but not knowing which were papers and which were gulls. Reaching for an expected pain, I had found only a numbness transcending pain and, later, Carina had come in and laid her hands on my shoulders and asked, her voice pale and anxious as her hands, 'Anything wrong?'

I do not mean to be disparaging when I refer to Carina in these terms. I am, after all, not much darker than her and although my hair is fair turned white and hers is white-blonde turned white, my body hair is as colourless and (as far as I am concerned) unflatteringly rare. I, too, can be nervy although not as pathologically so as Carina whose twitchiness sometimes reminds me of the dainty tremblings of a mouse – and that despite the fact that she moves her long, rather heavy bones in a manner that is unsettlingly male.

Do I love her? 'Love' is a word that frightens me in the way that these two letters frighten me and if I were to say 'yes', I would qualify that by adding that – in our case and from my side – love is an emotion too often threatened by ennui to attain to the grand passion for which I have long since ceased to hope.

Certainly, though, I loved her enough to be able to say, 'No, everything is fine,' and turn around and smile into the once so startling blue eyes that now – under certain lights and when looked at in a certain way – have faded into the almost as startling white stare of the blind.

Whether she believed me or not, I cannot say, and equally do I not know why I have bothered to even mention a wife, and a second one at that – the first having absconded to fleshlier fields a lifetime ago – who does not in any way figure in the now so distant and tangled happenings with which the letters deal. Or do I, indeed, know why and have I subconsciously allowed Carina to surface in a manner and image that have more to do with me than her and that will save me the pain of having to explain in so many words why, in those years of warping and war, an oddness in my psyche became set in stone?

Whatever the case, I am now back with the package and the letters, leaving Carina sleeping – or pretending to, she being disconcertingly perceptive at times – and no commonplace papers or gulls beyond the window to divert me: only a darkness that is as inward as it is outward as – yielding to the persuasion of the tide I thought had ebbed beyond recall – I turn to the package and start to unwrap it, then stop, not wanting this from him and as afraid of it as though it held his severed hand.

Or is this all fancifulness? Am I permitting a phantom a power that belongs to me alone? What relevance do they still have – a war that time has tamed into the damp squib of every other war, a love whose strangeness is best left buried where it lies?

Haplessly, unable to resist, I listen for the nightingale that will never sing again, hear only the screaming of an ambulance or a patrol car, a woman crying to deaf ears of a murder or a raping in a lane, and lower my face into the emptiness of my hands.

---

I am lying on the only patch of improbable grass in a corner of the camp. Balding in parts, overgrown in others, generally neglected and forlorn, it is none the less grass, gentle to the touch, sweet on the tongue. The odd wild flower glows like a light left on under the alien sun.

I am not alone. Bodies, ranging from teak to whiteworm, lie scattered at angles as though a bomb had flung them there. As at a signal, conversations swell to a low, communal hum hardly distinguishable from that of the darting bees, dwindle away into a silence in which I hear a plane droning somewhere high up, frustratingly free.

I am back in the narrow wadi sneaking down to the sea. I shelter under a rock's overhang, clutching the recently shunted-off-on-to-me Hotchkiss machine gun that I still do not fully understand. Peculiarly, I am alone but I know that in the wadis paralleling mine there is a bristling like cockroaches packing a crack in a wall of thousands of others who wait for the jesus of the ships that will never come. I have stared at the grain of the rock for so long that it has become a grain on the inside of my skull.

A bomber, pregnantly not ours, lumbers over the wadi on its way to the sea, its shadow huge on the ground, its belly seeming to skim rock, scrub, sand. I

dutifully pump the gun's last exotic rounds at it, mar-
velling that, for once, the gun does not jam. But there is
no flowering of the plane into flame, no gratifying hurtling of it into the glittering enamel of the sea, and I
stare after it as it rises into higher flight and am drained
as one who has milked his seed into his hand.

Later, a shell explodes near the sea, the sand and
the windless air deadening it into the slow-motion of a
dream, and the sun sets into the usual heedless blood-
hush of the sky.

I squat down beside the now useless gun, resting
my back against its stand, thinking I will not sleep, staring into the heart of darkness that is a night that may
not attain to any dawn. But I am wrong. There are
muted thunderings, stuttering rushes of nearer sound,
an occasional screaming of men or some persisting gull,
but I strangely sleep, as strangely do not dream, and am
woken – not by any uproar but a silence – to a sun still
far from where I have slumped down into the foetal coil.
I do not need any loud-hailer to tell me that the lines
are breached, that the sand is as ash under my feet.

Dully, I struggle up, still tripping over trailing sleep,
slop petrol over the gun and the truck of anti-gas equipment deeper in under the rock, curse all the courses at
Helwan that readied frightened men for the nightmare
that never was. The synthetics of the suits, gloves,
boots, intolerably flare.

Down at the dead end of the beach, I wash my face
in the tideless sea, stare out over the still darkened
warm-as-blood water to the skyline that has become a
cage's prohibitive ring, go back, then, to the higher,

now sunlit land where silent men are smashing rifles over rocks with the ferocity of those who wrestle serpents with their bare hands.

I pass what is clearly an officer's tent. It is dug in until only the ridge shows, neat steps leading down. Outside, a batman is washing a china plate, saucer, cup, his pug-dog peasant's face seemingly unconcerned, but it does not raise from its staring down at the trembling of the hands.

I pass another tent sunk in the sand. Again the ubiquitous robot's playing games, denying midnight now. Frenziedly the hands polish the buttons on an officer's tunic, button-stick inserted round the buttons so that the Brasso will not whiten the sullen cloth, bring upon the hands a comic wrath. The tunic's shoulder flaps flaunt a crown. I am thinking 'Christ!', beating back bile.

He is coming towards me, studying the anonymity of my fatigues, two pips glinting on his shoulders, sandy hair lifting in the awakening wind. The hair, the prissy pursing of the lips, the button mushroom eyes, warn of the worst of the breed and I snap him my still smart training college salute. He floppy-chops an arm back, barks, 'Unit and rank?'

I think to tell him I am Colonel this-or-that because how would he – now – ever find out otherwise, but the solemnness in the air like bells' dissuades me and I say, 'Sergeant. Second Divisional Headquarters. Sir!'

His eyes widen a little as he balances between surprise and what I suspect is a chronic tendency to disbelieve. 'Div. H.Q.? What do you do at Div. H.Q.?' There is a slight emphasis on the 'you'.

'Chemical Warfare Intelligence and Training. Sir!'

He is impressed and it shows in a slight inclining to me of stance and tone, and something like a greediness of the eyes, which makes no sense and which I dismiss as a stress-induced fancifulness of the mind.

'Do you want to hand yourself over like a sheep or make a break?' His voice is casual but his glance is sharp and I hear myself saying, 'Make a break,' even though previously there had been no thought of that in my mind. I am honest enough to admit that I am no hero and, even now, I am painfully aware that my excitement at the prospect of escape only slightly exceeds my congenital dread.

'Get in that truck then,' he says and indicates a battered three-tonner a few paces off. 'Where's your kit? Are you armed?'

'No kit, sir. No arms.' Even as the words still sound, I realize what I'm saying and I hump not my kit but my shame as I for the first time am faced by the fact that I never even thought of retrieving my kit from the anti-gas truck before I set the latter alight. As I said, I'm no hero and more likely to be stood against a wall than paraded for a gong, but he does not seem to mind, even nods, and I get into the truck and see that there are already others in it, lying flat, face down. Surely veterans, these, because they have lined the sides of the truck with the kitbags that *they* did not forget to bring, and another spider of fear scuttles up my spine as I understand – as I should have at the start – that they are braced for the crossfire that is already raging in my mind.

It would take but a step and a jump to again quit the truck, but I stay put and we are off, the truck weaving and rattling over the moonscape of the land, roiling up a hot white dust that settles in our hair, eyes, clothes, till we look like labourers in a cement factory coming off shift, and the knotting in me slowly slackens as there is still no shot or shout.

Then, without warning, we stop, the suddenness of it sliding us around like loose cargo on a canting ship, and the cab door slams and the lieutenant is shouting to us to leave the truck, hands raised. And we stand up, but don't raise our hands because we don't know what the shit he is on about, and the Jerries are ringing us round and the lieutenant is proffering his revolver to the brass in charge. But the brass waves it aside and the lieutenant turns to us and smiles, but there is nothing behind the button mushroom eyes and I know the meaning of betrayal and the rottenness that slinks in the flesh and breath of men.

'Come,' says the lieutenant. Then, patronizingly: 'We could never have got through, anyway.'

'And you knew that,' says the hulk with a beard beside me and a gun seems to flow into an extension of his hand, but his aim does not match the buccaneer beard and the lieutenant stares, chalk-faced and open-mouthed, as his shoulder shatters and the revolver farts a useless round into the sand.

The brass fires then and the hulk's face explodes, splattering me with blood and bone, and I lean over the truck's side and hurl up the supper I never had. Then the Jerries post a guard over us, gun drawn, and another gets into the cab beside the driver and the truck turns around and heads back into the dying town.

The lieutenant does not look back as the grey, stolid shapes close round him and I unashamedly claim the hulk's kit as my own and, upending his water bottle into my hand, cleanse my face and fatigues as best I can.

'Anybody lying here?' asks a pommy voice, referring to the narrow space on my left, and I open my eyes, but the sun is level with them now, blinding them, and I close them again and say, 'No.'

As expected, he takes the space without any further asking my leave, which would have been unnatural any-way in a place where anything unclaimed is everyone's prey, and I am only surprised that he had anything at all to say before he flopped himself down. His shoulder lightly brushes mine and I wince aside, not only be-cause I dislike poms, but because I have never been one for touching or being touched and, as a prisoner, I have been leant upon, trodden on, shoved all possible ways, with a frequency and vehemence that should see me through for the rest of whatever days are still mine. Also, he smells of soap, the overly scented yet almost frothless shit that one can sometimes beg or buy off a guard, and his shoulder is wet as though he has just crouch-bathed under one of the rows of taps in the open-ended shelter across the way.

I almost grow curious enough to turn around and look at him, but the sun is a gold leadenness in my limbs and I am back under that other sun as the Jerries add us to the biblical multitude that waits, not for any

Saviour, but for the older than that assembling of the enslaved, the time-before-time's smashing of the rebellious knee.

Actually, the conqueror turns out to be not at all like a royal Caesar or a rapacious Genghis Khan. Or should that be the other way around? Flanked by his panzers in his one overt try for histrionics and his face shrouded in the shadow cast by his cap, he speaks to us as one who too, dixie in his hand, stands in the queue when grub is up. We are, he assures us, lions (which, secretly and guiltily, we know we are not), but our officers are donkeys (which, most passionately, we know but too well), and a sigh like a wind in ripening wheat runs through us as we stand, belly to spine, locked in our adoration of this new god of war.

Not me, though. I am still seeing the lieutenant turning to us with his savouring smile of a little boy who pulls wings off flies and I am wondering what other and less pleasing agenda lies behind this companionable charade. And this mistrust is still prowling in me when a guy I know I know, but cannot at once place, comes up to me, humping his kit, sweat like a wounding under his arms, and says, 'I am from Div. H.Q. Aren't you?'

I look at him and nearly say, 'No,' because, one, I'm by nature a loner and my one-man job as the anti-gas freak has allowed me to indulge that up to now, and, two, this ou looks like he's going to make more of a loner of me after the first few exchanges about the nothing we share.

It's not that he *looks* all that bad. He's got this hook of a nose that reminds me of Issy Kapelowitz who was in our class at school, but I don't think he's a Yid because (unless he's a convert which only happens about once in a trillion years) there's a crucifix slung about his neck and, if you're asking me, it's ivory and he had better watch it or his parting from it is liable to be the brand of sweet sorrow he could well do without. His hair (what I can see of it under the dust) is brown and soft and more wavy than curled, and his brow is high (which does not necessarily mean that he has sense) and his chin juts (which does not necessarily mean that he is anything other than several kinds of an obstinate cunt).

His eyes, though, hold no ambivalence, interpret all else. Sunk deep in his skull, ringed by the bruises of a sleepless night, crinkled at the corners as though he laughs a lot or is a lot older than his flawless, clearly still natural teeth would have me believe, they are gentle – and conciliatory – and understanding – and every other damned innocuous quality that can sometimes so set my teeth on edge.

No, even with those eyes, his face is not intolerable, and his body is not laden with any belly and his legs go down straight and his arms, though no weightlifter's, are reasonably muscled and male. What *does* put me off are his *movements*: the little almost dancing steps he takes even when, supposedly, he is standing still, the delicate, frenetic gestures of his hands, the almost womanliness of him that threatens to touch – and touch – and *touch* – and I have already told of my feelings concerning *that*.

But then I look around me at the facelessness of the

crowd, the namelessness of it because there are so many to name, the stemming of us into this sweating, defecating mass by the single thin wire strung on makeshift posts pushed into the dispassionate sand; and the alienness of it all, of this scarred and dying world that holds nothing of the green exhilaration of my own heart's land, overwhelms even my solitariness and I look at him with something of a despairing and say, 'Yes, I'm from Div. H.Q.'

'I *knew* I'd seen you there!' he exclaims and his hands flutter like exuberant wings. 'I was a clerk in Intelligence. Typing and files. That sort of thing. What did you do?'

'Nothing much,' I lie. 'Emptying the generals' piss-pots most of the time.'

'Oh,' he says, a little thrown. 'But you are joking, aren't you now?' Then: 'Well, I think we chaps from Div. must stick together, don't you? At the moment I feel more like a child out of school than anything else and yesterday I quite sinfully enjoyed destroying all those stuffy files! But the feeling won't last because God alone knows where to from here. So,' and he thrusts out his hand, 'my name is Douglas – Douglas Summerfield. What is yours?'

'Tom – Tom Smith,' I say, struggling to get my hand back from his lingering clasp and naming my names as coarsely as I can in the hope that this will emphasize their commonness as opposed to the grandiloquence of his and so, from the start, abort a relationship upon which he seems ferociously intent, but from which my entire ego quails. I do have enough of a conscience left, however, to remember with some measure of guilt that the names on my birth certificate (and which I hardly ever spell out to anyone) are Thomas Aloysius Smythe.

The small, mean ploy fails. When I sit down on the dead hulk's kit, he sits down on his – next to me – and talks and talks, not irrelevantly or even tediously, but with a bright hungering for communication with – grappling to – another that bewilders me and draws me even deeper into a shell which he does not seem able to sense is there. Or does he and is it that which is spurring him on to ever more determined efforts to break me down?

There *are* moments, always brief, when he falls silent, takes a rosary from a button-down pocket of the tunic with its three stripes of the rank that we share and, running the rosary through his fingers, mutters under his breath with an intensity that unsettles me even more than the usual prattling of his tongue. And sometimes a sudden surging of the crowd will separate us and I will try to slip away from him through the bodies standing densely packed as mealies in a field, but always, somehow, he finds me again, either suddenly reappearing at my side, fine white teeth smiling and glad, or waving to me over the intervening heads like – I savagely think – a drowning clown or a tart desperate for trade.

Later in the day, the Jerries begin to truck us out of the temporary camp, travelling in slow convoy along the coastal road, the sea sometimes seen, sometimes only the salt of it crying 'Here!', and Douglas is again right there beside me in the truck, having held onto my arm with a bruising stubbornness throughout the crazed battling to get aboard. Why, I am wondering, did we so object to being left behind when, so Jerry tells us, we will tomorrow morning be handed over to the Ites who, we are assured, are something else again?

Dusk shading into night, the convoy stops as at a sign and the trucks melt into the side of the road. Ours crashes in under a low, almost leafless tree and the driver-guard whisks a camouflage net over the still protruding bonnet with the deftness of an old angler casting his line. Why, I do not know, because the sky has been clear of our planes all day. Have we still *got* any planes? Are the Jerries, the Ites and us all that is left of humankind? Where are the *wogs* to whom this soil belongs?

I get off, Douglas shadowing me – who else? – stare out over the flat endlessness the other side of the road, this solitary tree. Ancient flint glints in the half-light, the earth seems tinged with as old a blood, stubborn scrub starts up out of it like terrified hair and I am crying inside. Douglas, clinging to my profile, puts out a mothering hand, but I strike it aside and he exasperatingly smiles, nodding that he understands, and I come closer to prayer, fiercely, entreatingly, wishing him gone.

Astonishingly, the driver pours water from a jerry can into a canvas basin on a collapsible stand, invites us to wash our faces and hands, pantomiming what he means when his tongue fails. Warily as beasts too many traps have scarred, we edge closer, do as he says, but quickly, knowing that our necks are achingly exposed, and he fetches some cup-sized cans from somewhere in

the cab, not fearing that we might cut and run —
where to, anyway? — and begins to open them, not with
a bayonet, story-book style, but with a civilized tin-
opener that stabs me with thoughts of other places,
other times, as poignantly as it punctures the cans.

Then he hands us each an opened can, pantomiming
'Eat!' and I see that the cans contain chunks of a grainy,
grey meat in a splash of thin and oily slop, and I take
out a pinch of the meat with cautious fingers and taste
it, and it is as though I had never known a tasting
tongue before, and I bolt the meat and slurp up the
slop with all the passion of the hunger I had forgotten
my belly held. And Douglas, forever vigilant, looks at
with me with as passionate a pitying and hands me the
still uneaten half of his can, saying he is not hungry,
and I am sure he is lying and make to hand the can
back, but then think, as much of irritation as of hunger
overcoming me, 'What the fuck! If he wants to be a
prick, then *let* him!' and the Jerry picks up our two
empty cans and puts them with the other empties into
a sack and throws the sack into the cab, asking nothing
of us, more captive than conqueror and a *kind* man
who does not wish that we litter this small refuge that
none of us might ever again have reason to disturb.

Is it his kindness — or Douglas'? — that, too late,
shames me, turning the meat in my belly into the dead
flesh that it is as we lie down to sleep, I in the hulk's
greatcoat, Douglas beside me in a waterproof, the rest
variously huddled as the earth cools down with the suddenness of a switched-off stove? Quietly, I turn my
head. Douglas is asleep, lying on his back, his mouth

slightly opened, his breath even and slow, the hands with which he earlier counted his beads composed, the almost frenziedness of his waking self subsumed by the vulnerability of the inward child. Am I too intolerant of him? Should I cut the relationship and have done? Is 'relationship' not too strong a word? Can there *be* a relationship between the pursuer and the pursued?

I turn my head the other way, quickly now, aware of a rustling of wind or sand. The driver, unsleeping, is standing there, on guard and armed. His shape is very black, very tall, against the nearing, plunging, shower of the stars; his face, in profile, has a noble flow. Enemy and killer, yet there is a grace in him, a youthfulness and urgency that is as beautiful as it is animal and male, and I fall asleep against my will, knowing that he is there.

I wake up, once, before we must. He is still on guard, but standing at a different angle to where I lie. A misshapen moon is now low in the sky. I do not know if it is rising or setting, suddenly do not even know where we are, never having been further than where we lost the war. Long shadows reach for me as though I am the last of living flesh. A bird or beast horribly howls. I am floating again on a lambent, tideless sea where, a millennium ago, we swam under a risen moon, our limbs' pale tentacles seeking our beginnings in our ends.

At first light, Douglas is shaking me and we are all rising and looking past each other like dead men. Even Douglas, sensing our sombreness, spares me the usual bonhomie, and the driver sets up the basin again and we wash, distasteful of ourselves as though, in the night, we had consorted with a foulness primal as the sand. And the driver hands us each a crooked doorstep of black bread, indicating that he is sorry that he cannot give more, and in the clear betraying dawn I see that he is not at all tall, and there is a scar running from the corner of an eye to under the chin and his eyes are old and stunned from having seen too much too soon.

Douglas has readied his kit – and mine – and is now standing staring in the direction of the barely audible sea, fingering his beads and muttering what I have learned are 'Hail Marys', and, although I say nothing, having been taught respect for other people's faiths, I wish he would stop because, to me, prayers are a private affair and he is as embarrassing to me as though I had come upon him with his pants down and shitting behind one of these stones.

Maybe Douglas has a point, though, because he is just dropping the beads back into his pocket when the Jerry points to dust-covered truck after ditto-covered truck rounding the far western bend of the road and says 'Mussolinis' as though the word leaves a bad taste on his tongue. Then, his eyes gravely compassionate, he makes this-way-that motions with his hands that indicate a switching-round and my heart is darting in the cage of my throat and the bread in my belly is a black pregnancy of unease.

'Hey, Yank! You got a watch? I get you cheese and chocolate for watch.'

Where I am lying is next to the highwire fence and the speaker is so close that almost I feel his breath on my cheek. But I don't turn my head to look at him because I know who it is. It's the particularly scruffy little Ite guard with a face like the mummy walks again, his eyes alone belying that with their glitter like needles and the quickness of spiders on the run. To him, all prisoners are Yanks and have watches all the time and, like me, are suckers for chocolate and cheese, and his breaking in on my thoughts so peculiarly on cue worries the little extra-sensory worm I inherited through my mother's genes.

'Fuck off!' I say and turn my back on him and the bolt of his rifle clicks as he screams, 'You fuck me? I fuck you!' but I know he will not shoot and the ou beside me laughs an honest laugh that I could like, but Douglas has already taken his place in the ramshackle Ite truck rattling its way westwards under a lowering sun.

That night, we are herded into a cemetery with a fence around it that is as impregnable as any prison's, and although I am aware of random lights filtering through inadequate blackout shields, there does not seem to be any ongoing activity save ours and the night is as unidentifiably about us as the middle sea. The graves are clearly those of wogs, and believing wogs at that because the mounds of earth are mostly unadorned in compliance with a faith as austere as the desert in which it was first proclaimed, and, in the still moonless night, I stumble and fall as from a reaching of hands and know a horror at our desecration that no agnostic should. Douglas, though, is undisturbed, ensconced as he is behind the barricade of his beads.

'Herding' is too harsh a word? Hardly so. Jerry was right about the Ites. Runts in ragged uniforms that uniformly don't fit, egged on by foppish officers who porcinely, tediously scream, they flail into us with boots, fists, rifle-butts, their zest the tired simulations of children playing a game long since no longer new.

I am generalizing the way xenophobes do? Perhaps I will ask myself that question, maybe even answer it, in some later, more gracious time − supposing, of course, that such a time can ever again *be* − but at the moment, in a night that never ends, my only philosophy is that of the living who would not be dead as these we are now trampling under their crumbling mounds.

As the incoming trucks disgorge more and more of us into the burial ground's inelastic space, cramming us against each other and the dangerous discomfort of the barbed wire fence, I say to myself that this cannot go on and, when the moon at last rises, I see from Douglas' face that he is telling himself the same thing, his eyes disbelieving and stunned, but − and this stays with me − his soft, garrulous mouth set as tightly as mine in his determination to stay alive. Hell, I am thinking, he is *not* all piss and wind.

Sometime in time's long standing still, stasis is reached as we stare with faces pressed against even the inside of the only gate and the guards know that to open it would be to unleash an onrush as involuntary as the bursting of a dam. I am locked into the arse before me as though I sodomized it and am locked from behind in as final a negation of the privacy of my flesh, and Douglas' hip is jutting into mine like a broken-off iron and my own bones are lattices of pain that hold back my knotting body's unending scream.

Somebody farts, raucously as a wordless shout, and a gusting stench of urine and shit tells of another who, despairing and ashamed, has let slip the beast of his need. But nobody laughs and I am thinking this can only be the Hell in which I have never believed, and, as we suddenly, and as though impelled by a single consciousness, tilt gatewards, then spinecrackingly whip back, there are howls as of souls in torment – and garglings into silences that as terribly sound.

Incredibly, then, there is light in the east and the trucks are stuttering into life, and the gate is crashing open and there is an exploding out into a measureless space. But before I reach the gate, my one boot sinks into a crackling softness that I cannot bring myself to look down at because I know it is a crushed-dead man, and it is only when we have been cuffed back into our truck that I lift up the boot and uncontrollably shudder as I see that it is splattered with blood and fragments of what could be flesh and bone. Wordlessly, Douglas gropes around on the truck's littered floor and comes up with a piece of paper and – as wordlessly and expressionlessly, and without any by-my-leave – lifts up my foot and wipes the boot clean.

The truck jerks itself off and trundles past a meagre complex of prefabs lining a side track that leads back onto the coast road, and there is a silence between Douglas and me that, for once, drags on with no sign that Douglas will be the first to speak.

But I am burdened by something I must ask and, at last, I do: 'What was your job before the war?'

He looks at me, surprised by this first ever question from my side. 'A male nurse. Why?'

'Just asking,' I say and watch the ball of paper,

bloodied by my boot, rolling around. But my mind is changing gears with the grinding reluctance of the truck that, like all the Ite trucks, seems likely to at any moment topple over and die. Which is an unfortunate image after what I have just been through.

The salt flats glitter all the way to the blue smear of the sea and the sun is not much past noon when the convoy suddenly stops and we scramble out of the trucks to the usual accompaniment of clicking rifle-bolts and hysterical yells. Bewilderedly, we mill about, ant-like under the vast brass of the sky, wondering why, and Douglas puts on his Intelligence cap and says maybe there's been an operational shift, that our forces have regrouped and are now retaking the conquered sand. I snort at that though, secretly, I hope, and one of the others from our truck irritably asks why the Ites can never do anything without kicking up such a fucking fuss, and Douglas rather meanderingly says that the little dark ones are from the south and the taller, paler ones – who seem to comprise their officer class – are from the north and the two are as different from one another as vinegar from wine. Which is a rather refreshing variation of the usual chalk-and-cheese cliché and again the gears are shifting in my brain.

The Ites are not prone to giving us toilet breaks, compelling us to, en route, piss or shit from the inside looking out, which usually means to jut buttocks or cocks over the trucks' sides and do our thing to the Ites' inexhaustible – and adolescent – delight. So, now we decide that this unexpected stop is to be our toilet break and there is a general pissing and dropping of pants where we stand, but the Ites will have none of it and furiously begin to drive us deeper into the flats.

As in the just-past night, only terror tinged with a dull anger stirs in us as the normally ludicrous takes on a shape of nightmare under even so high and revealing a sun, and no laughter moves in us with its saving grace as we watch the beatings as of beasts of those still struggling to free themselves from the hobbles of their pants, and the face of our Jerry driver floats out before me like the fragment of a dream already ages old, and I reach out as to a lost and redeeming friend, but the emptiness in me is the emptier for its finding only the Now.

The ground is firm enough under our boots, but there is a hollow ring to it as of water warningly close, and I am reckoning it will be bitter and salt as the crystals strewn like some malignant frost over the curiously ochre earth. Also, there are shallow depressions of cracking mud that tell of water in some other time, a surging, perhaps, of a capricious tide. The occasional scrub is twisted and black as though a fire had swept it or an enervating poison gripped its roots, and the even scarcer grass is cancerous and brittle as a dying man's hair, and I am hearing the usual silence that even our frenetic trampling cannot shatter or obscure.

Is this a place for a killing, a cutting off from them of a flesh that is conquered but for which they have no use? The thought is upon me like an assassin in a private place and I look at Douglas and, for the first time, there is a true communion between us as I see that he is thinking the same thing though not wanting to, and he is shaking his head and assuring, 'No. It *is* just an operational trick. You'll see. They'll be moving us on again soon,' but there is a stridency to what he is saying of one who secretly does not believe.

He is as right as he is wrong. The sun sets – and rises and sets – and still we live, although dying is all we think about, strive against, as no summons to move on comes, and the skeletons we pretended we did not have begin to show, and our lips crack like the old mud's heaving apart, and our tongues are the tumescences our loins no longer need.

In a stray quirk of fertility, near where the trucks still wait under their camouflage nets for the planes that never fly, is a spring that surfaces into a wide, shallow pool, then again runs underground. The pool is ringed with grass of an almost unbearably brilliant green, and there are small honey-scented flowers and hovering, doubtlessly rowdy, bees. We passed it with a quick wonder when we were driven into the flats; now we stare at it all the time, quivering with the intensity of dogs held back from a bitch in heat as the Ites man the machine guns they have set up round the pool and occasionally, with the casual sadism of children, splash themselves with water, empty their water bottles onto the burning iron of the earth. Someone who called the guns' bluff is still lying out there, minus his face, silent under the shifting coverlet of the flies.

At noon of the third day, the sun is a struck gong in our skulls. A second man, lured by the shimmering siren of the pool, weaves out towards the guns. They shoot him too, the reports flat as a toy pistol's popped cork, no bird starting in terror from the crackling salt.

We rise, then, as one, mindlessly march to a beat of the blood only we hear, a heedlessness of death our desperate armour for the insane. As from some other earth, we apprehend the flawed flats' shuddering under our steps, hear the senseless whisperings of our swollen tongues, knot our every tissue against the bullets that must surely come.

But the guns are silent and the Ites are hauling them back to the trucks as they concede us the pool, and we are a mob again, breaking ranks, rushing upon the spring with an incontinence that strips us of the brief dignity we had donned. Douglas, his face raptor as the rest, beak of a nose scything the air, mouth set as a trap, starts from my side with a fleetness I would never have guessed at and wriggles his length into the writhing mass of bodies covering the pool, his jostlings ruthless and maddened as any, and I cannot decide whether I am feeling smugness at his degradation or disappointment and shame.

When at last our thirst is stilled and some are vomiting, their bellies dangerously ballooned, there is as little left of the spring as of our pride. The grass is crushed, the flowers effaced without trace, the once crystal water turned to a tired sludge, and we trudge spiritlessly back to the trucks when summoned, no thought in us of escape, leaving behind us a scarring we now inescapably bear in our own selves.

Douglas is strangely silent as we again trundle westwards, his beads slipping, dutifully, through his fingers, but his lips unmoving and his mind patently elsewhere.

'I suppose you don't think much of me any more,'

he at last says, his tone wistful and his eyes misty with a not-quite-tearfulness that irritates me as profoundly as the beads.

'What the fuck are you talking about?' I snap, laying on the harshness, partly because I *am* feeling pissed off – although I do not quite know why – and partly because I suspect that any softness on my part will have him blubbering on my shoulder like a little boy. Or should that be 'little girl'?

'About the way I behaved at the spring,' he says, his fingers juggling the beads almost frantically now, aggravating my mood.

'What makes you think you behaved any differently from everybody else? Including me?'

'Yes, but I left you behind. I never once thought about you. I thought only of myself.'

'For Chrissakes!' I explode in a whisper so as not to share this slush with the rest of the truck. '*Will* you stop mothering me as though I were a little kid? You're not *that* old! And anyway, I don't need you. I don't need *anybody*. I've looked after myself nearly all of my goddam life!'

'You said "mothering",' he cuts in. 'Why did you say "*mothering*"? Do you think I'm one of *those*?'

'Those what?' I nag, though I know perfectly well what he means.

But he doesn't answer that; only stares at the blank, cab side of the truck as though there's nothing there. Then he turns me right around, the whine in his voice quite gone.

'I can't help how I am. I have got this way of moving

and speaking, and I have got this way of *caring* about people. That's why I became a male nurse and why I was glad to get into H.Q. and handle files instead of guns. But I have a wife and son whom I try not to think about all the time and I'm hoping that these,' and he flips the beads, 'will see to it that I get back to them one day.'

'So?' I ask, fending him off, but sensing I'm going to lose.

'So I'm a talking fool who was hoping to find, at least, a friend to go with me into the God knows how many years yet of *this*,' and he gestures about the truck with those too graceful hands. 'So do you want me to sit somewhere else from now on?'

'It's OK,' I say, my voice curt and dismissive, but he seems to understand that I am only being me.

A shadow falls across me, clotting the slits of sun that still anchor me to the present, and Douglas' voice says, 'Tom,' and I ask, 'What?' and Douglas asks if I have seen his rosary, and I say it was lying on his bedding and he probably folded it up into his blankets as he has done so many times before. And Douglas says, 'Of course!' and the sun is shining in the slits again.

'He one of the funnies?' asks the pommy voice close to my left ear, and I know exactly what is meant by 'funnies' and am not amused. But I don't work up a sweat about it either because everybody reacts to Douglas in that way the first time around, then ends up liking him for the guileless fool that he seems.

So I pretend that I had not heard, but the voice persists, 'He your mate?' and there is a slight emphasis on the 'mate' that does get my goat and I mumble, 'Mind your own business,' and would take the matter further, but I am already an ocean away as the convoy finally stops in the late afternoon of the following day and we are left to infest the multitude of brown army tents that have been erected for us on a waste of sand white as bone.

The sea is near – its tang enticing on the windless, still torrid air – and, for a moment, the sand beneath my boots is beach sand, and I am a boy again. Also there is a city – seemingly so close that a stone, thrown at it, would rebound, clattering, from the nearest wall. But that is a trick of light and air and actually it is a long walk away, sunken in a depression beside the sea, only the upper floors of the taller buildings and the domes and minarets of the many mosques towering up with a shining, magical whiteness that matches our own still pristine sand.

But there is illusion upon illusion because, as the light fades and the shadows gather like mauve water in every angle and hollow, I begin to see that it is a paint-less city with many paneless windows and fault-lines in the walls that tell of bombs in the days – the years? – when our planes still had a say in the skies. But then a muezzin in a minaret is calling the always absent wogs to prayer and there is a sweetness and foreverness about it that heals, and hope is walking back to me like some old friend with a half-forgotten face – or should that be half a face? – and I watch with something like satisfac-tion as Douglas lays out our private space in a tent that must surely house a hundred sleeping in the round.

Douglas is still 'mothering' me? I have given in to

him like the macho weakling that I am? Yes, but the 'weakness' is more like a rare kindness in *me*, I having come to understand that, for Douglas, to not mother someone is to not breathe. And then, this first night in a place with a roof of sorts and a double body's length of sand we can call 'his' and 'mine', there is an appearance of domesticity, of a *home*, and a home is a bipolar thing, balanced between his yin and my yang.

All of which is, of course, a load of bull and is quickly shown to be so. A rumour floats – and refuses to blow away – that any day, without warning, we will be shipped off to Mussoliniland, and, at once, the illusion of permanence – or even semi-permanence – is shattered and we stand again amongst the graves and the sand between the tents is a slyness of salt that has claimed us for its own.

As though to drive the point home, the Ites' taunting of us resumes in a manner that is frighteningly known. Once a day – usually when the sun is at its highest and we are stripped to the underpants many of us no longer have – the water trailers circle the camp in round after round of mindless sadism, water sloshing and chuckling with a delicious liquidness that unfailingly lures us out to the milling and yelling of the captive beasts at feeding time that we have become. Only then do the trailers take up their stations about the camp and we complete our degradation as we jostle and bicker – and all too often bloodily fight – in a queueless rush to fill our water bottles and whatever other containers we have been able to scrounge.

There is also a minor, more in-the-face, version of

the game that so turns the Ites on, which sends murder bellowing through my brain. An Ite guard, prowling the camp's perimeters, looks out for the last of our watches flashing on some innocent's arm, offers a whole multi-litre can of water for the watch, brings the can, slopping water onto the sand, takes the watch, then upends the can, laughing like fuck as the innocent, more often than not, breaks down and weeps like some little kid that's seen his world end before its time.

Whichever version of the game, it is then that we again foul the clear pool of our human genes, and the sand beneath our boots bares its myriad teeth of bitter salt and I am thinking it would have been best if they had shot us back there and buried us, or left us to rot, in the last shreds of a dignity we were never fit to wear.

And then there is the food – the one ladle a day equals a three-quarter dixie of strangely grey macaroni drenched with an oily soup, two bread rolls no bigger than the standard 'English' bun and a to-be-saved and delicately, lingeringly eaten two-inch cube of oddly superior cheese. Sufficient to sustain life if not spirit, this is a diet that encourages the body to a new equilibrium of skin and bone, limits conversation to fantasies about food, goads whatever spirit *is* still left into the vitriolic intolerance of each other of too many scorpions in a jar, and often I go out and sit and stare at the city whose name I now know but will not disclose because that will destroy its timelessness, as it will destroy the timelessness of all that is happening here.

It is not surprising, then, that this morning I have

this trouble with the guy that sleeps next to Douglas and me. He was a war correspondent for a Jo'burg paper – or so he says – and is an almost runt with a long, narrow face and a matching nose that twitches in tune with a world of stimuli he alone prowls. The once rakish moustache now straggles and is stippling out to its subsuming by as flourishing and bristling a beard, and the eyes, black and liquid as olives, scuttle far back in sockets ringed with shadows heavy as mascara on a whore.

His eyes are like that because he masturbates, masturbates with a frequency and ferocity that is neither hilarious nor titillating, merely drearily, sickeningly obscene. Lying on his side, jerking and whimpering like a ridden-over dog, he sometimes milks that pitiful cock twice in one day and I am having difficulty remembering *any* day when he left the fucking thing alone. Even between wanks, he's juggling his balls or fiddling with his foreskin, his mood petulant as a kid that wants to play after the other kid's called it a day, and I say to Douglas that, Jesus, this has got to stop, and he says, no, to leave the 'poor man' alone because he's seen this before and it's like a disease.

This morning, though, confrontation comes at us like life skidding on a wet road. It is still early and the tent is mostly quiet, sleeping being one way of not being here, and I am not listening to Douglas fingering his beads and whispering his Ave Marias, and I am *trying* to not listen to the wanker having it off with his cock. But as his grappling goes on and on, it begins to seep through to me that something is wrong, that he is weakening without anything happening, that the starving body is at last rebelling against the lust that is more in his mind than in his loins.

So it is that suddenly he slumps and a long groan drags out of him like the final exhalation of a dying man and I'm thinking, 'Thank Christ, maybe there will be one nut less here from now on,' but then he is whipping round and glaring at Douglas who is lying between him and me and his eyes are white with hatred and rage. 'It is *you!*' he hisses. 'You with those goddam beads that's spoiling it for me!' and he lunges to snatch the rosary, but I am over Douglas and on him, and we are entwined and rolling, but skeletally and slowly, our breaths snuffling and noisy as pigs', our bodies the leaden baggage in a nightmare that will not end. But then his genitals, balls swinging beneath the sad, shortening erection, have flopped through the split crotch of his underpants, are dangling within the reach of my hand, and I grasp them, wholly and viciously, driven by a sadism born of my own deprivation and despair.

'No!' he shrieks on a note so high that the sleepers wake as one, and I loose him and he lies, coiled and sobbing, his hand clutching his groin as though it was his smashed, favourite toy, and I am expecting Douglas to chide me for treating the 'poor man' so, but he is looking at me with glowing eyes, the womanishness in him strutting as never before.

'Shut up!' I snarl as though he had spoken aloud, and turn over and, amazingly, sleep, and when I again wake up, the wanker is gone and Douglas, still proudly glancing at me from the sides of his eyes, says he walked out, muttering, an hour ago, and late in the afternoon a guard comes to fetch his kit and tells us he will not be back because he was flashing his cock to all the guards about the camp and complaining that it had died, so they took him to the Ite doc who pronounced him crazy as a coot and is having him sent to an asylum in the city where he can play with himself for the rest of the war.

Douglas does, then, again speak of him as 'that poor man' but not too forcefully so, and I try to feel a proper guilt for the part I have played in putting the guy where he now is, but then think, fuck it, he's probably better off there and, in any case, I am as edgy as a fox when it comes to probing into motivations that may turn out to be quite other than they seem.

Douglas, though, has no problems with that. To him, I am just the selfless friend who leapt to his defence in the hour of his need, and this discovery of so unexpected a depth in me encourages him to complain that I have never told him anything about myself, whereas he has told me all about his sterling silver upbringing and his as sterling silver, still living and doting mum and dad, and has shown me photos of his wife and kid, she a clearly breathy dumpling of a woman who would drive me crazy in a week and the kid looking just like all the other kids I have ever known. So I tell him my mother was a gypsy who told fortunes in a tent she pitched in her flat in Hillbrow, and my father did time for flogging stolen watches in the street, and, when they died early on in my life, I paid my way through university with the loot I earned at night from running with a gang whose mark is still on my shoulder, and I show him what looks like a branding with a hot iron, and he looks at me disbelievingly and a little affronted, although it just might all be true.

'I got to piss,' says the guy I had forgotten was still there. 'Keep my place for me, will you?' and I nod without looking, listening as he swishes away through the grass, then no longer listening as we clamber out of the stripped shell of the cargo boat and the first stones from the crowds lining the streets of the southernmost Ite town thud into us with a hating that hurts the heart rather than the bones. I, like the most of us, walk hunched and flinching, pretending I do not hear the cries that accompany the stones and that clearly are curses because, here and there, I can make out the few dirty words that are the only Ite-speak that I know. Douglas, though, strides out with a certain majesty, rosary plainly in his hands, and no stones seem to be striking him, which could be a miracle but is more likely to be because the Ites are also Catholics and are not sure whether he is one of ours or one of theirs, and inevitably – and hopefully unworthily – the thought comes that there could be one smart cookie behind the beads.

But now there is a settling down beside me again and a proffering of thanks to prove that the right man is back, and I am thinking that I must have dozed off there because I never heard him coming through the grass. And I am remembering also that he said he was going for a piss and for the rest of my life, hearing that word – or 'shit' – I will be back in the ship that brought us from a sand I had never thought I could love to a land lush with leaves and holy bells as a new Eden over-lying Hell.

And always, then, that horror in me of a whole flesh that sleeps, then wakes to a rotting in a sudden leper's skin.

Truth is, I do not *want* to think about that ship, any-time, anywhere. But, however briefly, I *have* to because it is a link in a sequence of events that I sense is rushing me to an end that is as unpredictable yet ordained as that of a car whose brakes have failed on a long hill. With each thinking back, the aversion grows and the de-tails become less, the conscious me beavering the easily movable items such as the days at sea, faces that crowded us, guards that yelled, into the lumber-room of the subconscious where, hopefully, everything will one day lie mumbling but chained.

At the moment, though, it is as I said – the operative words are still vividly 'shit' and 'piss' and I was of the very many who had the shits the day we boarded the ship. Not Douglas, though – male nurses being exempt from indignities such as a runny gut. We thought we were being clever when we battled our way to the front of the queue. Would this not, then, ensure us a choice space on deck? Instead, we found ourselves at the bot-tom of the booming, cavernous hull, beside us a single iron ladder that reared up past the encircling higher decks to a hatchway that was closed most of the time but which, when not, held a circlet of sky as distant and surreal as the mouth of a well. Up this, by day and at night when the hull was lit by the minimum of naked

bulbs that cast more shadows than light, passed the despairing, embattled sufferers of dysentery or diarrhoea.
The hatchway would open and close, open and close,
and the number of times that I managed to win through
and, as in the case of the trucks in the desert, jut cock
and arse over the swaying ship's rail and try to shit out
the porcupine of pain that was the cramp in my gut
while the guard shrieked at me to have done, is one of
the details that my mind mercifully no longer yields.

Most of the time, though, we never made it to the
top and would hang like shot birds from the ladder's
rungs as we let slip our shit and the accompanying piss,
not, for that brief moment, caring about the profanities
below, but shamelessly, as in an orgasm, revelling in the
collapse of the anus' clench, its bestial abandonment to
the bowel's need. Being at the foot of the ladder, we
would have been hardest hit, but Douglas, with something of the ruthlessness that had so shamed him on the
flats but which now did him proud, nagged for and
found a more distant space for us and there, each time I
shat my pants, took them from me and, with the remote impassiveness of the nurse, washed them as best
he could in the pool of sea water that mysteriously
sloshed in the deepest part of the ship's hull.

At night, we would lie, sleepless, the sea writhing beneath us like some monstrous serpent that at any moment would break through the ship's frail hide, the
meagre rations and as little water they had issued us before we embarked dwindling and unceasingly tempting
us to finish them off at one go, and, all about us, even
now sneaking from every pore of our skins, shit and

piss, and piss and shit, and only Douglas' face, and his hands washing my pants, worth time's sparing of them and the reason for my remembering anything at all.

But now the Now is reaching through to me like the sun to a diver cleaving up to the top strata of the pool, and the images that are the links I seek are fewer and scattered as we move up from the first southern squat to this far northern camp ringed by hills and clangorous with bells.

Still in the south, the Ites discover – or did he some-how leak it to them? – that Douglas was a clerk at Div., and he swings it so that I become his assistant and we sit sorting prisoners' records at the old infirmary amongst the olives and oleanders, and Douglas, with ad-mirable and patriotic amorality, insists that we do next to nothing for our double ration of macaroni and rolls.

And there is the time at the stop half-way to here when the Ite guard holds me down on the stout-legged wooden stool and the Ite doctor, scorning anaesthetics, yanks out the last of my lower back teeth, abscess and all, and leaves it to Douglas to stop me bleeding to death and deaden my pain with tablets he says he filched from the infirmary down south; and there is the night at the same place when we catch the ou who has been stealing our boots and flogging them to the Ites, and we dunk him up to over his head in the pit latrine that's full to the brink with shit, and he crawls out of there with only his white eyes and red tongue showing, and I feel an irrational pity and something of his guilt, but, this time, morality wins and Douglas – the prim

Douglas of old – says, 'Serves him right,' and, for a moment, seems almost ready to say, 'Serves him *fucking* well right.'

Then it is that I sleep, an illusion of stability enfolding me in this, at last, established camp – and something of a domesticity too as my thoughts stay focused on Douglas who has grown on me from the so-small seed of my tolerance and for whom I have come to feel an affection that may not be passionate, but is rooted in the respect due to a solid and honourable man.

———

'Hey! Wake up!' says the voice, loudly, in my left ear and I start up out of a scattering of dream, my mind snatching at the dwindling fragments till they whimper and are gone.

The eyes so close to mine are black and intense though, I suspect, normally lazy with smile, and they are very slightly squint which lends them a mischievousness that may or may not be only in my own mind.

'Why?' I ask of them, my tone oafish and irritable and the irritability tilting towards open anger at this ou's breaking into me time after time.

'You were talking in your sleep.'

'So? What's it to you if I do or I don't?'

'You were talking *loud*. Lots could hear.' Then he waits, but I don't respond.

'You were also crying,' he adds, a note of triumph in his voice as of one who's played an ace.

'Don't talk shit,' I say, but it might just be true and I'm not as certain as I sound.

'Is so. Look,' and I flinch as a finger touches my cheek and he holds it up, shining wet.

'It's sweat!' I snap, but I'm uncomfortably aware that the rest of me – which means all save my privates that are lost somewhere in one of the hulk's long short pants – would wet no finger eager to prove a point.

That he is aware of this I do not doubt, his eyes almost tangibly travelling my body's length, and I ready myself to slap away any further violations of my private space. But he merely grins, not nastily or mockingly, but good-naturedly, almost approvingly, as though he applauded me for so stoutly carrying on lying in the face of truth.

'OK, have it your own way,' he says with no suggestion of petulance or spite, and links his hands behind his neck, his elbow nagging my shoulder, and stares up at a small, slow cloud forming and dissolving in an otherwise empty sky, his face distant and inward as though I am no longer there.

But now I am intrigued by his unexpectedly conceding me victory, even though the issue could not have been a more niggling one. Or am I wrong? Is this, in fact, a gesture of some grace on his part? Is he not so much conceding me victory as respecting my wish – macho adult male that supposedly I am – to not be caught snivelling, even in my sleep, like some little kid who still thinks it's just for pissing through?

Covertly, I study him, slewing only my eyes. His hair is black, springy, tightly curled, capping his head like a Renaissance cherub's or an old Greek bust of a beautiful boy. Blessedly, though, his face is neither beautiful nor a boy's. The nose is pug, the chin a shade pushy, the lips yielding and mobile, yet wholly male, the brow low – which last, I have long since learned, has nothing to do with intelligence or the lack of it, is merely the reverse of high.

Lower down is the body of a man who works at it – the breasts at the apex before masculinity becomes womanishness, the nipples pert and clear, the hair in the armpits tufting and lush, as lush a body-hair flowing with the flat belly down into the generous crotch, the tautly powerful thighs.

It is only then that I articulate it to myself that he has been lying beside me in the nude. Christ! I think, wanker No 2; and think it again with a quite puzzling and personal disappointment when he reaches down and scratches in the thick thatch of the pubic hair. But, seeming to sense what I am thinking, he suddenly turns his head, catching me unawares, and asks, 'Is this worrying you?'

I play it dumb. 'Is what worrying me?'

'Me lying here with nothing on.'

Now I turn my earlier answer round. 'What's it to me what you wear or don't?'

His lips twist, but tolerantly as though he has been through it all before. 'OK. So it worries you,' and he gropes beneath his buttocks and drags out a quite astonishingly clean pair of underpants and wriggles himself in. Then he turns to me and his eyes seem blacker than when first seen, and brighter, and yet impenetrable as shades. 'Don't get any wrong ideas. I'm married though no kid yet. But lots of time still, me reckoning I'm about your age. I was a boxer and I was good and I aim to go on being good when I get home. So I got a nice body – *got* to have – so I got to *keep* it nice. Even in a shit dump like this. Run, do P.T., get the sun on me – *all* of me. Sun's good for the body. But I don't *walk around* like I just been born, and nobody gets to touch me down there,' and he gestures at his crotch. 'Only my wife.'

I say to myself that I don't believe this; then I explode. 'Who the hell are you to talk to me about getting wrong ideas? Why don't you say straight out what you mean? Just now you just about called my mate a queer because he's funny with his hands, and he a married man like you and *with* a kid, if you please! Maybe it's *you* that's the queer – you with your body that turns you on like it's your whore and don't touch it there or … What makes you think I want to touch it anywhere? Why don't you haul your fucking body some place else and have it off with it where it's all yours?' And nearly I add, 'And I hate poms,' but somehow I just don't get that far.

There is a long silence then in which I wait – a tension in me that I am loath to admit – for him to do what I ill-temperedly certainly would, but he at last merely turns his head to me and says with a directness that disarms, 'I'm sorry about your mate. I was wrong.'

Again I am nonplussed by a yielding I did not expect, and I mumble an awkward something and turn my back on him, seeking refuge in a withdrawal of sorts. But there is still a question that has to be asked and answered and I ask it, feeling more than a little guilty and defensively annoyed: 'What did I say in my sleep?'

'Enough,' he says, the one word neither taunting nor amused, and I wait for more, but nothing comes.

'Well, what was it?' I prod, getting edgy now at having to so beg.

For a moment I think he has not heard me, then he thrashes round to face my back and says, his voice low, 'Not saying.'

'But why?' I burst out. 'Don't I have a right to my own words?'

'Not saying,' he repeats. Then adds, 'Not saying because what you said is why I am still lying here after you bad-mouthed me like you did; so now if I tell you what it is, I'll be telling you more about *myself* than I'd like.'

His tone leaves me in no doubt that, this time, he will not yield, and I am perversely pleased by that and, indeed, suddenly and startlingly aware that if he had again given way, he would now have confronted more than my merely physical spine. However, I cannot resist still saying, 'You are weird,' but the words hold no barb and, with the intuitiveness of the dead gypsy in my genes, I sense that he knows that and is drawn.

'No weirder than you,' he retorts, then, switching tracks, adds, 'They call me Danny. What do they grab you by?' and I tell him and he says 'Tom' as though savouring it, then asks where I'm from, and I tell him, and he says he's from a village that's a nothing and he and his wife and his mum live in an on-its-last-legs cottage that was all that his dad left when he died.

'How long you been in this dump?' I tell him six months and forestall him by saying that he must be one of the rookie prisoners they sent up from down south last week.

He looks at me like I'm clairvoyant and, for the first time, I laugh. 'It's easy. Your hair needs trimming but it's still not a nest and your beard's only begun.'

'Now wait a minute! You bulling me now? OK, so your mate looks like he's a guru come down from his squat, but you look like my kind. That's why I came to lie by you. The rest of them here look like all the grand-dads I ever seen. Real creepy, them.'

'Watch it! You will be just as creepy soon. Anyway, Douglas – that's my mate – *wants* to grow a beard.' Abruptly – and with an acuteness that disturbs – I am asking myself why? *He one of the funnies?* The words resonate in me as though I am hearing them for the first time. Does he think a beard will make him look more of a man? Determinedly I wrestle the thought away. 'But I feel like you. I don't want to look like a granddad before my time.'

'You got a razor then?'

'Hell, no. This is just like *any* fucking jail. You die how, when, *they* want you to. Not by you cutting your – or someone else's – throat. So once a week I go to the shed alongside the gate where you come in and get the worst of it taken off. The theatre crowd hang out there. Stage musicals, plays. The Ites smaak musicals and plays. Opening nights, all the front seats must be re-served for the commandant and the other Ite brass. They get almost human then. Shout, clap, carry on like little kids. So when the producer asks for the cutthroat and shears, the commandant lets him have them because he understands *all* the actors on the stage can't have beards or heads that look like that old guy's that slept a hundred years,' and I'm about to add – big joke, this! – what about the guys that must shave their legs and arms and truss up their balls so's they can play the parts of the women we do not have, but a red light flashes on, loud as a scream, and I simply say, 'So Tony, the producer, lets me pretty up there free of charge.'

'He's your friend?' The voice behind me is carefully saying nothing at all and I know I am going to try and walk softly even though I am wondering why the hell I *should*?

'No, only Douglas is my friend. But Tony's OK,' which he *is* though everybody knows he's also a raving queer.

'Then why the favours?' persists the voice, shading now from offhand into chill, and I know walking softly is going to be no way to go.

'Because you'll be seeing me in one of his plays soon. That is, if you're interested enough to come.'

He says nothing, only grunts as he heaves himself back onto his back and I see red. 'Come off it!' I quietly rage, not wanting those around us to hear. 'Not everybody on the stage is a poof. Or do you think *I'm* a poof, in which case,' and now I also turn back onto my back, 'nice body or not, get off its lovely arse and come at me like a man. This is *prison*, pal, and you live and let live; and you *entertain* yourself as best you can or go mad; and if a poof can put on a play better than you can, then you *let* the poof do it and stop acting like an old woman who's got a hand up her leg.'

Then I wait, my heart and gut flopping over like a fish that's hooked because this is a *boxer* and, if he *does* get up, he's going to do, at least, that Ite dentist's job on my teeth and I have got enough problems with them as it is. But he merely asks, his tone as back to normal as though he hasn't heard a thing I have said, 'What is "smaak"?' and I am scrabbling to get my bearings before I remember and say, '"like". The Ites *like* musicals and plays,' and he nods with a solemnness that betrays that he is not as comfortable as he pretends, then goes on, 'So you are saying I have to go on the stage to get my hair cut?' and suddenly we are both laughing, he whooping it up in a way that means *now* it is OK again.

But he is serious about the haircut, so I explain, 'You can *pay* for a haircut. We've got real barbers here. We've got real just about *anything* here. You go two huts up from the theatre and you'll find the pint-sized shack where the barbers will do anything you ask except give you a shampoo. The Ites not only know about it — they *run* it. In the mornings, they hand the barbers the cutthroats, scissors, clippers, you name it, and in the evenings they check that everything's still there, then take it all away again. Not forgetting, of course, the commandant's share of the poor guys' earnings for the day.'

'Yes, but *how* am I going to pay? I've no money on me!'

'Didn't they hand you any Red Cross grub and smokes when you first came?' He nods. 'Do you smoke?' He says no. 'So what did you do with the cigarettes?'

'I stashed them. I always stash anything I don't need because you never know.'

'You're damned right you never know. You hang onto those beauties because they'll buy you your haircut and a span of other things you're going to want.'

He stares at me, perplexed. 'Look, they're your *money*, man! In this camp, there are those who smoke and those that don't. Those that smoke like to smoke more than they like to eat, so they will flog you their Red Cross grub – or even the camp swill – for cigarettes, and you grow fat while they grow thin like those seven lean kine the Bible goes on about. This is a cruel world, pal. Then there are those who like to both smoke *and* eat. They are the gambling boys – the Mafia. Every day, all day, sometimes half the night, they play cards. For what? Cigarettes. Play till they are rich beyond any decent slob's dreams. Then they smoke some of the cigarettes, spend some to buy extra food, spend some more when they hire serfs to do the chores they are now too busy gambling to do themselves. This is where my mate and I come in. We are the working class. Every Monday, all Monday, we wash gamblers' clothes, working our way up to someday being Mafia of our own, only we will have done it with our hands instead of the brains we don't have. It's a whole new system that's growing here, pal.' Almost I say his name, getting carried away, but restrain myself in time. 'No banks, no taxes, no interest, no inflation, not even a printing press to print more dough. But it works. Don't ask me why.'

'Because the Red Cross is printing your dough,' he at once says, and I mull that over and think, Christ, this guy's no dope. 'Also,' he adds, 'judging by those shorts you're wearing, all that fucking around with other people's crappy underpants doesn't seem to be paying off the way you say.'

'Capitalists are not made in six months,' I protest, but there is an approving in his voice that I do not miss. 'As for the shorts...' and I tell him about the hulk and how I got to wear the shorts.

'Sad,' he says and it is not just a word. 'I was in the tank corps. What were you?'

'A machine gunner,' I half-lie, not caring overmuch that I do; only hoping that he will not ask more questions and that *Douglas* will not someday let the rat out of the bag. A survivor with an attitude, I am not going to lightly admit that I was mostly an anti-gas wimp at H.Q.

But his mind is already back with himself. 'I must run now,' he says, jumping up. 'Keep my place if you stay on.' But then he turns back and looks at me appraisingly, then nods as if satisfied and goes, and I am envying him the hair on his back as on his front and the mahogany-dark tan that makes me wonder if his stock is not Celtic Welsh rather than Saxon pom?

Also I'm thinking that Douglas will be wondering why I'm lying here for so long, but there is a dissatisfaction in me, a feeling that some climactic point has not

yet been reached, *must* still be reached, and I watch
for him to, time after time, briefly appear in an arc of
the camp's perimeter nearest to where I am. Of one
thing I *am* certain, however, and that is that, as he
rounds the camp with a seemingly unvarying fluidity
and grace, he is not conscious of anything save the
honed and seamless machine that is his flesh and his
driving need to subject it to his will.

But, slowly, as I wait for him to finish and return, a
question is forming in me like the cloud that earlier
built in a windless air – a question that, unbelievably, I
did not at the time ask and that now seems laden with
the electricity of meaning of a balance that a breath
could swing either way.

And then he *is* returning, but from a quite different
direction from the one in which he left, a smallish glass
bottle glinting in his hand, and his breathing is deep but
steady and his body sleek as a seal's with sweat and his
step proud. Also, there is a towel about his neck, which
means that he must have called in at his hut, and now
he stops at the ablution block and lays the bottle down
out of reach of the splash of the taps, and strips off his
underpants and crouches down under a tap.

Then he dries himself, slips the underpants back on,
picks up the bottle and comes across to me. 'You still
here?' he asks as though he did not expect me to be,
and I take my cue from that and say, yes, I wanted to
go but I have thought of a question that I should have
asked him before and I would like to ask it now.

'OK,' he says and sits down flat, uncorking the bottle
and shaking a splash of what smells like liniment into a

palm. 'Not much left,' he mutters more to himself than me and begins to rub the oil into his calves and thighs. Then he starts kneading the small of his back with his oily hands, looking up at me with steady, pre-occupied eyes, saying, 'Need the wife for this'; then adds, 'What's the question?' taking me by surprise.

Certain now that he is listening, I suddenly feel fool-ish, even reluctant to go on, but there is no question of *not* going on, so I hear myself say, my voice gruffer than I had planned, 'Why is it, after you had been here a whole week, that you knew nothing about the way things here are run? Shit, I talked to you like on a guided tour and I could see that, to you, it was all new. Didn't you or your friends *ask around*?'

For a long moment, he stares at me, his hands strug-gling with his back and a new question nagging at me that I am *not* going to ask because I am not looking for the job, namely, why doesn't he ask me to rub his back for him like most other guys would? Or did he see me flinch when his finger touched my cheek?

'I don't *have* any friends here,' he says at last, his voice disinterested and remote.

'Well, couldn't *you* then have asked around?'

Again he takes forever to reply. 'I'm not a talking man.'

'Well, you did all right with me today. Was I an ex-ception to the rule?'

'Depends,' he says and grins, showing all of his white, square teeth, and I leave, mumbling something fuzzy, fleeing as from a thrashing between trees.

You can lead me blindfolded into our hut at a time when, say, everybody is out and standing in a queue, and whip off the blindfold and I will at once know it is our hut. Big deal? Yes, because the Prussian-grey, dull-windowed prefabs are not only outwardly the same but – to the first glance of the uninitiated – inwardly even more chillingly so. But I am not fazed by every hut's seemingly uniform debris as from a blast: the scattering of garments, mostly tattered and soiled, the dixies, mugs, spoons, whether washed or unwashed, the desperate substitutes contrived by ingenious or blundering hands, the tumblings of blankets and greatcoats in the three-tiered bunks even long after noon, the kitbags dangling from nails driven into the bunks, the ash, food scraps, mud, trampled into a patina of filth as ineradicable as the grain of the floors, the indefatigable flies.

But there is more, much more, to every hut than that. There is also a *spirit*, as there is a spirit to every human shape, individual and unique and compounded of the sweat, sperm, blood, fears, hopes, insanities or profundities, of the two hundred of us allotted to each hut's precisely calculated space, the whole honeycombed with aisles down which only the skeletal sidle with ease. It is this spirit's embracing me, enticing me into the manifold foetors of its crotch, that enables me to say this is our hut even before the blindfold is removed; and it is hastening to me again now, loud, amoral, yet curiously comforting as even the harshest of homes can be, as I come in from the long lying in the sun.

Douglas is part of this home. Take him away, I

think, and there will be a wound that messily bleeds, that nothing heals. What am I trying to defend? Off balance as one in sudden darkness or blinding light, I stand at the bottom of the aisle leading up to our two bunks, watch him furiously flouncing around. In this slough of inertia and decay, he alone finds something with which to murder time, is forever scrubbing utensils with sand till they shine, whisking the broom of useless twigs down our aisle, making and remaking his bed (and sometimes mine), speed-reading the weightiest book the camp library can provide, prowling, eager for bargains, the one-man, one-box food stalls where the non-smokers with a talent for trade set out their Red Cross cans of margarine, jam or Spam.

And, above all, vigorously pestering the old bastard with the belligerent beard and dead-fish eyes who occupies the bunk between my top and Douglas' bottom one and doggedly refuses to be bludgeoned into exchanging his squat for mine. This disrupter of our familial life distresses Douglas more than he does me, which the latter, I suspect, senses because he communicates when Douglas is not there, telling me – among much else – that he was a staff sergeant in Stores and hinting without provoking that he thinks Douglas is more than a little mad. For which he is not to be too greatly blamed.

This rank business is no minor issue because this is a camp for NCOs who are not allowed to volunteer to work for the enemy on pain of being court-martialled for treason after the war, which means that our interloper can slightly pull rank and probably is already doing just that by staying where he is. Sad, in a way, this senior in every hut becoming hut boss and the most senior of the whole camp becoming our link with the Ite brass, which means he gets to tell us what shit *they* want us to do next. Like a fowl with its head chopped off doing its shadow dance of life-after-death? What, I wonder, is Danny's rank, then wonder why I should quite so sharply want to know, and carry on edging up the aisle.

Now Douglas is clambering down from my bunk, deliberately almost treading on the glowering enemy beneath, and I come up close and ask, 'Hey, what are you doing up there?'

Startled, he hits the floor and turns and says, badly lying as any child, 'Just tidying up your bunk,' but I look at him and he looks away and I say, 'I told you before, let it *be*. You can't always have everything your own way.'

He shuffles his feet, then, and I know he is blushing somewhere under the professorial beard and that he will again be pestering the stubborn-as-he, pernicious presence in the middle bunk the moment I am no longer there.

'What's for lunch?' I then ask, and I'm not meaning the once-a-day dixie of camp swill and two buns per man which is just about due, the hut headman already standing ready to give the word when our hut's number is called and we must nip down to the gate to take our turn.

'I bought a tin of Spam from that chap with one eye who came over with us on the boat. He's opened a stall near the toilets with just about nothing to sell and I thought we should give him a hand. OK?'

'How much did you pay?'

'Thirty smokes,' which is expensive, but I don't moan because the Red Cross parcels are late this month, which means that the stalls' stocks are running low and it is the sellers who are calling the shots right now.

Then Douglas is looking at me more closely and I know why. 'But Tommy!' he exclaims so that half the hut can hear and the little devil of my hatred of such diminutives is right there beside me, slipping his thin blade into my side. 'Where *have* you been?'

'What do you mean where have I been? You saw me lying out there in the sun, didn't you?'

'Yes, but for so *long*? Boy! are you going to *peel*!'

'I fell asleep,' I say, and the little devil with the knife asks why the lie?

Then the headman gives the word and I grab our dixies and fetch the swill, and, when I get back, Douglas has sliced the Spam sliver-thin and separated the slices into two exactly equal shares, and I mash my share into my swill and Douglas does the same with his, and we sit eating, huddled out of sight in his bunk because still so many of us have only the swill, and Douglas is prattling non-stop about trivialities, but I hardly hear him because of the little devil still asking me why the lie?

After lunch, Douglas says that if we are going to have tea, I will have to fix our blower-stove which is acting up, and I examine it and see that the fan that whirls round on a spindle when you crank it and blows air like a bellows in a forge onto the bed of wood-chips that we are sometimes allowed to collect on the surrounding hills – or the undersized, way-below-grade coals that the Ites dump on our side of the fence for us to use – is wobbling and knocking against the casing of the hammered-flat Red Cross food cans, and I fix it and we go out to the brewing site under the camp's only tree and brew two pinches of the black flakes, scarce as gold, that used to be everyman's humble tea.

Which is one helluva sentence, I know, but this is one helluva gadget that doesn't exist anywhere in the still free world. Light, limbless and so portable that you can carry it with one hand, it can boil water, warm up food (or, on a cold day, your hands), as efficiently and quickly as any four-legged, sturdily-planted, civilized stove. And, yes, I did make it myself, Douglas being like a man without hands when it comes to working with wire and tin, but I did not *invent* – nor do I know who did – this one of uncounted thousands of its kin that whirr and puff under dixies of swill or tea or frying Red Cross Spam and are, to me, the crowning demonstration of how the human slob got to be the smartest bully of them all.

After tea, I stash the blower while Douglas rinses the dixie and mugs, then lie down on my bunk and look down at Douglas flipping through the pages of a hefty tome from the library about chemical fertilizers, and when I ask him how he can be interested in such shit, he says he's not reading the book because of the fertilizers but because the fertilizers remind him of fields and flowers and stuff, and I think, 'As fucking weird as *him*,' and get restless and clamber down from the bunk and say I'm going to Tony for a haircut and shave.

'But you're only due tomorrow,' Douglas reminds, dragging himself away from the book.

'I know, but I don't think Tony will mind.'

'Tony will eat you alive when he sees what you've done to your face,' and Douglas aims his long nose back at the page and I think, 'Why can't he, just for once, say something *coarse* like *grab you by the balls?*' and take the long way round to the theatre, zigzagging through the blowers at the brewing site – 'Will somebody show Danny how to make him a blower so that he can brew the tea that no pom can do without?' – and meander further through the huts' humming like hives, looking in at each in a manner that is not me at all.

'I am bored,' I say to myself, almost in surprise, the theatre now clearly seen, and try to bluff myself that this is just the usual camp malaise, but a more ruthless voice tells the truth and I am deeply shamed because he is a loyal and honourable man who is satisfied with the so very little that I give.

'Christ! What have you done to your face?' Tony howls, clever hazel eyes widening under the gold-rimmed pince-nez it is a wonder the Ites have not already swiped for the gold.

'Fell asleep in the sun,' I lie for the second time, and Tony shakes his hairless-as-an-egg head and the long melancholy of his face sets into an even more dolorous mould.

'But, Tom, you *know* the show's on in a week's

time. Why the fuck did you have to go lolling around in the sun at all? Have you forgotten that you're supposed to be a pasty-faced British subaltern in the mud and sleet of France in the Great War, not a Saharan legionnaire who's lost his way back to the fort? Do you think the Ites dish out greasepaint like they do their macaroni without cheese? How many sticks of the stuff do you think it is going to take before I get you back to looking what you are supposed to be?'

'Don't worry,' I mutter, feeling more than ever like a pissed-off family man with a shrew for a second wife. 'I will have peeled by then.'

Tony sniffs, twitching the small, fine-as-porcelain nose that complements the dashing smear of the moustache. 'Better do some praying that you are right.' Then, 'But why are you here now? Rehearsal's only at five.'

'I was hoping you would give me a shave and a trim.'

'That, too, is not down in *my* diary for now. It is for *tomorrow* if dementia is not already setting in.'

'I'm still hoping you'll give me a shave and a trim.' ('But why the hurry?' asks a Tom I flee. 'Why must it be *today*?')

Abruptly Tony smiles, baring his beaver-like front teeth, the dolour momentarily gone. 'Sit down, you bloody serf,' he says, and I do so on the rather regal chair with arms that is reserved for this more mundane aspect of his art, and he knots a pleasantly clean cloth about my neck and begins to strop his cutthroat with the furious abandon of an assassin anticipating an enjoyable kill.

Tony – or so it is rumoured, he being as sensitive as women are supposed to be when it comes to his age – is in his late forties, but does not look all that much older than my still very early twenties, his spry, sinewy body possessing the agelessness of those in whom the grinning granddad lies dormant till the bones buckle under the load. In short, I could have been his son, which should be a guarantee of sorts, but I am always still wary of Tony, inwardly shrinking from his touch – as, indeed, though to a lesser extent, I do in the case of even heterosexual fussers with my hair. My reaction – or should that be obsession? – is all the more perverted for my knowing that Tony, being a poof with class, would never, without my asking him – which means never – take advantage of my defencelessness whilst in the chair and grab me where he must not, but no amount of reasoning with myself cures me of my cringe.

But he does take other liberties, such as: 'How's the wife?' he suddenly asks.

'Cut that, Tony! You know Douglas is not like that.'

'Like what? Give it a name, man. You are old enough to say the word.'

'And old enough to take out your teeth if you don't shut up,' I say, but there is no earnestness to it, we both knowing that this is only the usual bitter fun.

For a while he works on me as though I am a dummy under his hands. Then, 'You are such a waste.'

'What do you mean by that?'

'Nice body, trying-to-be-nice heart trying to be loyal. Such a waste.'

I know I should be getting angry now, that he is going too far, but his voice is sad.

'You don't like him, do you?' I ask instead, holding my tone steady as I can.

'It's not that I don't like him. I *hate* him.'

'But why?' And now I am too shocked to be annoyed. 'Because he is my friend?'

Now he again shows his teeth, but they are no longer a smile. 'Don't fancy yourself, kid. I don't care two fucks *who* is your friend.'

'Then *why*?' I again ask, uncomfortably aware that I have, indeed, fancied myself, made of myself a fool.

'Because he is like a sister that has left the tribe.' Then he whips off the cloth, says, 'Sweetest job in town,' and turns away, saying 'Bye,' and I thank him and make for the door, but he stops me and adds, 'Camel says to let you know he would like to be working on that portrait again,' and I nod, knowing what he means.

Camel is called 'Camel' because he *reminds* us of one, rather than actually *looks* like one – all long, arrhythmical bones that jangle and sway till you almost believe you can *see* the hump on his back that is not there. Add to that a beaten boxer's nose, ears that hungrily yearn, an alcoholic's flush – though no alcohol is to be had – and perennially blood-drenched eyes, and you have something of the ugliness of the circus sideshow that enthrals even as it repels.

So, having nothing better to do, I straight away make for his hut at the other end of the camp and find him sitting on his bunk, sketching heads without bodies and bodies without heads, the latter hung with genitals bursting with lust. Is he hetero or queer? His mannerisms are as unfortunate as Douglas', but whereas I know for certain that Douglas is straight, he never having made a wrong move, I'm not as certain about Camel who has the habit of looking at my fly as though unbuttoning it and whose sketches, like these, do little to swing the balance the other way.

Also, there is this business of the portrait of me which he offered to do and on which he has been working, off and on, for weeks without making much progress as far as I can see. I first turned down the offer, saying it was nonsensical to paint a portrait of a nothing like me, but then my not so very latent vanity, plus Tony's telling me that Camel was, of all things, an Aussie and a painter of some repute, seduced me into changing my mind and I have been spending endless hours in improbable postures while Camel paints my face and studies my groin.

I tell him Tony said I must come for another sitting and he stares at me as though I am flotsam from a ruined past, then says 'Ah!' as at a revelation and, seemingly irrelevantly, adds, 'Tony's changed you again,' as though that was a heinous crime, and I look at him bewilderedly and he says, 'Doesn't matter, though. I only want to do your left eye,' and angles my head to a hundredth position with his bony, broken-nailed hands, his breath malodorous as a drain.

Then he sets up his paints and home-made collapsible easel in the aisle, thus blocking all traffic, though no one seems to mind, and 'does' my left eye, his usually quivering hand knowledgeable and sure, and I ask if I can look at the painting and he stares at me as at one deranged, then shrugs, and I hate what I see.

'Why is my one eye squint and where is the skin on my face?'

Patiently, as to a child, he explains, 'The squint eye is your evil eye. We are both devil and angel, you know. And there is no skin on your face because I am not painting your skin. I am painting what is *under* your skin – the real you that you are not wanting me to see.'

'Looks more like a joint in a butcher's shop,' I sneeringly condemn, which waspishness does me little credit because he is, after all, doing it all for free. But he takes no offence, only looks at me a little pityingly, even shouts after me as I leave, 'That hunk who was lying beside you this morning – if you see him again, tell him I want to paint him too – in the altogether,' and, trying to make up for my just past boorishness, I nod that I will though I know that I won't, facing up at last to my day's several subterfuges and deceits.

———⟫●⟪———

I wake early, still depressed by the knowledge that the previous evening's rehearsal had been a flop. We fluffed our lines as though it was the first time round and went through the motions of passion with a spiritlessness that left Tony, literally, in tears. Fortunately, after the histrionics, he calmed down and said we were probably over-rehearsed, which was his fault and the next rehearsal would be the dress rehearsal the day before the show. But, this being my first time ever on the stage, the previous day's debacle stays with me as a warning of how easily the elaborate creature of deception that is a play can strip itself down to the nothing that is at the heart of all legerdemain. What, I ask myself, if that should happen in front of all those goons out there? — and I cower like a cornered beast under the howl of laughter I clearly hear.

But it is not only the rehearsal that is involved in my waking early and the mood that I am in. From the first day of our arrival here, the huts have hosted un-counted hordes of bedbugs, about which the Ites refuse to do anything and that, as soon as the lights are switched off, flood out of the joints of the bunks and even drop from the roofs with a sound like light rain. Then they feast on us with a ferociousness out of all proportion to their size, releasing their distinctive shel-lacky stench as we crush them between our nails, and there are mornings such as this when my harassed flesh can take no more and I writhe as upon a bed of tin-tacks, if not yet of nails.

There are also rumours of lice, Douglas swearing by all that's holy that he has caught the interloper checking on his crotch, and I point out to him that there could be a trillion other reasons for the poor guy doing this, but Douglas persists, motivated as much by spite as any fear for the purity of his own private parts. But I show only the fear as I now find *myself* covertly sifting through my pubic hair for the nits that will betray that a new pestilence prevails.

Finally, and for the first time in I don't know how long, I have dreamt an erotic dream that I am unable to recall, but that has left its sowing of sperm between my naked thighs – I, like most others, sleeping in the raw as the hot, dry summer drags on – and I hang my towel loosely about me and hurry to the ablution block where I wash off the sperm, being as shy of exposing my condition to Douglas as though I had spent the night with some whore.

After a glum tea, I ask Douglas, 'How's my face?' and he says, 'Horrible,' and I go out with a heavy heart to the tanning site, knowing there will be no tanning for me, but wanting to be there with an urgency I am reluctant to confront. Towel screening my face, I wait and time drags past me like a snake with a broken back and there is a leadenness in me as long as the snake, and I am starting to ask of myself what did I expect, when his shadow falls across me like the axing of my mood and I am ludicrously, honestly relieved.

'I went running first,' he says, not apologetically but merely as though it is a matter of some gravity that needs to be, at least, explained. But I am flowing with the current again and there is space for playing games. So I shrug my shoulders as though it is of no impor-tance to me that he be early or late, or even not come at all, and he looks at me with a speculativeness that is as penetrating as it is calm.

'I didn't know we had a date,' I say with a facetious-ness I at once detest, and see that he is dressed in only a boxer's shorts, and sweat is sheening him like a water, and the bare, demanding feet are gripping the earth with the tenacity of a tree.

But, apart from the level stare, he does not react,

simply says, 'I must shower,' and goes; then turns back, groping down the front of the shorts, and takes out a tightly folded square of cloth black as the shorts, and tosses it at me, it as wet with sweat as the hand. 'Doesn't fit me any more. Will you, though,' and ducks in under a tap, shorts and all.

I flap out what he has tossed and it is a replica of his shorts, clearly no longer his size and as clearly mine, and a tenderness as powerful as only tenderness is shakes me for an instant snatched from an Eden time. Then he's back, scattering water like a hosed-down hound, no towel for the drying of him, the sun to be doing that as he flops down on his back beside me, legs scissoring at some ghostly bicycle of the mind.

'Thanks for the shorts,' I say, my tongue difficult from long disuse when it comes to acknowledging favours done, my spirit equally recoiling from the debasement inherent in kissing the giving hand. 'But why *me*? Why not to anyone else you happened to talk to in the shithouse or under the taps?'

'You fishing?' he asks, his tone lazy, but his eyes alert. 'Maybe it's just because it embarrasses me when you look like you do and people think you're my mate. So do me a favour and don't grumble. Or do you want me to go and lie somewhere else?'

Again I shrug, a last of pride impelling me to the brink. 'It's up to you. I'm not your boss.'

'Nor me yours,' he snaps back. 'So shove the shorts up your arse if you want!' As quickly his anger dies. 'But why are you sitting here like some old biddy under her shawl? You hurt your head?'

For answer, drawing back now from the brink, I remove the towel.

'Jesus!' he yelps, pitiless with mirth. '*Have* you been *fried!*'

'Ja, go on! Laugh!' I complain, but beginning now to also laugh. 'The show I'm in is on next week and the producer's having pups because of the way I look. I'm not supposed to be sitting out here at all.'

All at once it is so quiet I can hear a gang of Italian sparrows bickering in the brewing site tree, and I dimly sense that I have said that which exposes me beyond recall.

'Then why *are* you sitting here, Tom?' and his voice is as triumphantly possessive of me as the gift of the shorts, and I draw the towel back over my head, confirming without words what he already knows and only then realizing that, for the first time, he has called me by my name.

'You married?' I shake my head, letting the towel hang. 'Tough. A man only gets to be his whole self when the old dick finds the right hole.'

I grab at the irritation that takes me out from under the towel. 'Come off it! You think I don't know what it's for? Maybe I been around more than you before we got in here.'

'Maybe,' and now he's doing the shrugging. 'But you're not listening. I said the *right* hole, not *any* hole. The right hole's when it's not just about getting the dick down.'

He has me by the balls and I know it and reach out to the sparrows, but, like all sparrows, particularly Ite sparrows, they don't stay in one place for long. Rumour has it that the Ites are so hard up for meat that they hunt even the wild birds and that is why the mornings have no morning sound.

Then he's off on another track. Or so it seems. 'Your mum and dad still around? I told you about mine.'

I look at him sharply, but nothing stirs. So I give him what I gave Douglas and he does not say anything disbelieving, just stares at me from the black silence of his eyes.

'You left something out,' he says when I finish, his tone accusatory, and something close to alarm moves in me because I know that I have. Then he adds, his eyes still meeting mine with an almost stubborn openness, 'I did too.'

The confessing of a complicity foxes me, and I look it and he says, 'You hated your dad like I did mine.'

I try to bluff, rearing back from an again threatening brink. 'What gives you the right to say that?'

'What you said in your dream.'

Now I am mortally afraid. '*What* did I say in that dream? Why must you be so secretive about the fucking thing?'

'I told you why, but maybe I must flash you a card now because it's getting to be not right for me to know so much about you and you still seeing only my skin.' For the drawing of a breath, he pauses, then he jumps, 'In your dream, you were telling your dad to stop doing something to you that mine used to do to me. And you're hating him for it though he's dead because he's mashed you all up inside. OK?'

An ant is struggling through the grass at my feet and I study it as though it is the most significant sighting of my life, then a wholly alien voice says, 'OK,' and I hear a snick as of a bonding leather's tightening one more notch, and he touches my knee with his hand and I start as at a reaching from another time, another flesh, and am ashamed.

Glancing aside, I see that his shorts have dried and at once know what I must say. 'You can take them off if you want.'

He does not pretend to not understand. 'You not minding any more?'

'*You* said I minded, not me. Maybe it's my potty training, but it's just not something *I* would do. That's all.'

'But you flash the old gonads every time you get under the tap. What's the difference then?'

'There *is* a difference then. It's like all of us sitting on that long seat over the shit pit. You sit down, maybe whistling a little to show you don't care, try not to fart too loud, *definitely* don't look at what the next guy's doing, just concentrate on being an animal all on your own.'

'Well, thank *you*!' and he grins, but the grin is plainly narked, as plainly pained. 'So I'm being an animal like I'm in a *show* just because I want to be brown all the way down?'

There is a silence in which still unsaid words jostle behind our tongues like surplus passengers trying to cram into an already-crowded train. What do I *really* want of him? Desperately, racing against the silence, against his quickening drawing away, I fling aside layer after layer of conservatism and pretentiousness, even downright lies, come at last to a kernel of ultimate mass that drags me to it, forces me to face it, though I would not have it so. Covertly I study him – sensing that he senses that I am – see, not the black boxer shorts, but a leprous whiteness of pampered skin, see a wildness of true innocence chained and tamed, say, 'Danny,' and he turns to me and I say, 'Take off the shorts,' and his eyes flicker out of focus as at a blow, and then a blackness beyond their blackness is gathering in them and he is raging as at the touch of a defiling hand.

'No!' I insist. '*No*! You do not understand,' and our eyes clash with the passionate intensity of the dumb and I shake a little as he slips out of the shorts, casually as though they were but a shirt or vest, and laughs, 'Jesus! I nearly clobbered you there!' but there is a brokenness to the laugh that wakes an echo in me that stays.

I am thinking I must leave now because I'm beginning to feel like a real rookie under the towel, but I fear that to summarily break off after the just past wordless crisis would give the impression of a fleeing as from a scream, and I cast around for a way to return to the mundane. It is then that I remember my concern about a blower-stove. 'You made you a blower yet?' I ask, reining my tone in as best I know how.

'You mean those things like fire engines without wheels that you guys wank around with all day?'

'None other,' I affirm, his description easing me into an easy laugh.

'Wouldn't know where to start,' he confesses without shame. 'Where do I get tools and stuff?'

'Have you got empty Red Cross tins?'

'Some. I shoved them under my bunk. I got a bottom bunk, thank Christ.'

'You give me your hut number and I'll come tomorrow after chow and show you how to hammer out the tins and fix them together to make you a stove.'

He looks at me with an unexpected hesitancy and I think, 'What *now*?' Then he says, 'Maybe I should tell you I'm only a one-striper, but you, I'm guessing, are a sergeant or a staff.'

'A sergeant. But what's that got to do with me making you a stove?'

'Well, we poms have got iron up our arse when it comes to ranks and my hut's all poms. Sergeants and above, which means I get to eat a lot of shit most times. So they might think you're a one-striper too or, if they find out the truth, that you're a traitor to your rank, and either way you're not going to feel much like you're home from home.'

But I say, 'Fuck them!' and he tells me the number of the hut and I leave him with the conscious unceremoniousness of old friends, then have to hurry back to pick up my shorts, and Danny is already deeply asleep, his breathing light and even as an untroubled child's.

There is nothing of the child about the genitals, though. Adult, aggressive, shrewd, they lie sprawled as though scattered by a heedless hand and I am considering them fully for the first time. But they do not add to any intimacy between us, alienate, rather, because they

are the forbiddenness in even this sad Eden, the ultimately untouchable zone before which our shared
maleness wields as ultimate a blade. Does the sun, as
the sun will, already bloat the listless penis, persuading
it to that other shape that will shame him when he
wakes, arouse a laughter in those who see? Should I lay
the shorts beside him over his loins, act the possessive –
jealous? – male, risk his anger for a meddling that may
not be needed, is motivated by impulses I would prefer
stayed unnamed?

I leave him as he is, face a second crisis of the absurd
as I near our hut, the shorts he has given me in my
hand. What will *Douglas* think of such a gift? Save for
his hostility towards the interloper between our bunks,
he has always seemed magnanimous and tolerant, one
who, to myself, I have summarized as *big*, but now I
am no longer sure and the shorts hang heavily as infi-
delity from my hand. Should I throw them away? The
thought is obscene and I sleepwalk into the hut, still
not knowing what to say.

'What have we there?' Douglas asks with an immediacy that does not reassure, long nose hoping for a surprising, voice singsong with the chirpiness that can
either aggravate or sustain.

Infamously, my tongue finds a lie. 'A pair of shorts.
Found them lying near the taps. Just my size, too.'

'But you are not going to *keep* them, are you?'
Douglas is all set to moralize.

'Well, why not? I asked all around where I picked
them up, but everybody was being honest john and said
they weren't theirs. What more can I do?'

Douglas ponders this. 'Not much, I suppose. We can hardly ask *everybody* in the camp, can we now?' Never before has the plural 'we' worked such havoc with my nerves.

Grunting, not trusting myself with more, I stash the shorts, noting that they are still damp with his sweat, thinking of him sleeping out there in the sun.

———

It is as Danny had warned. All the heads seem to swing as one when I enter his hut to start work on the stove. 'Like a cockless ox wandered in amongst the bulls,' I think, and note with satisfaction that – the spit-and-polish reputation notwithstanding – their hut is no better than my own. Less pleasingly, it also smells as I would have expected a pom hut to smell – airless, incestuous and mean. As I have said before, I don't like poms, Danny being the exception that still doesn't change the way I feel.

Then he takes out the tins and I get down to showing him how. Also, I'm making like I'm a single-striper like him and enjoying the added intimacy this brings, and we hammer and chatter with a deliberate obnoxiousness and I sense an aloneness slipping out of him and standing aside a little as is the way of the shadow in every man. He is quick to learn and his hands, unlike Douglas', are cunning and sure and, in the end, it is me that is sitting back spouting the shit while he carries on, his face absorbed as a watchmaker tweezering springs.

Late in the afternoon of the second day, the blower is ready to blow. A motley beast of various strains of tin, its lines are none the less racy and proud, and it gusts up a fine dust from the hut's floor when we crank the fan round, and Danny cannot wait for us to try it out, so I ask him if he still has any tea, and he drags out the Red Cross box and I see that the still unopened packets of tea and sugar and a tin of condensed milk are all that is left and think, a heavy pity unsettling me, 'Christ! a *pom* that has not had any tea all this time!'

He had also stashed his dixie in the box and I note that it has been washed, although not as obsessively and shinily so as Douglas does his and, more often than not, mine, and this earns him full marks because Douglas' fussiness is sometimes funniness and sometimes an irritation that drives me into a not always silent walking up the walls. So we go down to the brewing site and brew us a dixie of tea, adding sugar and milk and drinking in turn from the dixie until only the leaves are left and they to be saved for a second brewing and maybe even a third, and Danny is whooping it up with that sometimes boyishness that is most luminously him, but the tea is tasting like piss to me because I am remembering that all but empty Red Cross food box and knowing with a pitiless clarity that his ability to keep his flesh on his bones is so much less than Douglas' and mine. What, I am asking myself, can I do to help him stave off the surfacing skull? But there is no answer to that. Only the certainty that the question, rowelling me like a demon, is on my back to stay.

At one stage, a plan born of desperation comes to me and I put it to Douglas that we broaden the infrastructure of our laundry business by taking in an extra partner or two. That way, I am thinking, *Danny's* survival base will be widened, if not ours, and I couch the proposal in the plural rather than the singular so as to lend it an aura of objectiveness that will allay any suspicions Douglas may come to harbour that I have a particular individual in mind. Why I should so fear that Douglas will turn the proposal down should I play open cards is clearly due to a sense of guilt which, in its turn, is by *no* means so clear, and I am equally at a loss as to why I should now, in effect, be suspecting the usually generous and jovial Douglas of a jealousy and possessiveness he has never so far betrayed? Or has he, only I chose to not see?

Whatever the case, I am honest enough to admit to the naked cynicism of my approach – a cynicism that is compounded by my choosing to speak to Douglas while he is counting his beads and is, presumably, on some kind of a spiritual high. Should I feel shame? Of course I should, but this vision I have of a half-starved Danny circling the camp with a condemned man's leaden tread, underpants or boxer shorts flabbily about his grown-bony thighs, overrides all else, turns our jazzed-up camp swill into an abomination on my tongue.

I am, indeed, the manger under Douglas' dog. 'What do we want more partners for?' he demands with a sharpness, almost dread, that is totally unlike the Douglas I thought I knew. 'Aren't we doing well enough on our own? Why drag in someone we don't even know and, ten to one, have him muck up our whole routine? Or have you already *found* some wonderboy who's going to show us how it's done?'

The single word, 'wonderboy', is the key to the true

nature of the passion confronting me in the guise of a drab economic rebuke, and I watch as the fingers fondling the beads accelerate their fingering as though in response to that passion's quickening beat. Anger rises in me then, blindly, blunderingly, seeking words, and Douglas is suddenly, shockingly, other – stares, smells, differently as a dead man, and the blade of my tongue wants to sever him from me beyond all recall. But the past months of shared suffering, his grappling with my shit in the belly of the boat, the innumerable lesser kindnesses that were hardly less, cry out to me with something of the chill remonstrance of birds in the deep night, of the night's as-chiding wind; and the clicking beads have us back gathering wood on the abutting hill, and, guard in the rear, we are passing the tiny church with its peeling pink walls, and a straw-stuffed Madonna is sprawled out on the ground for repairs, throat slit, head lolling and loose, glass eyes glaring in mindless pain, and, in a flash of sight beyond sight, I am seeing Douglas and the doll as one.

'Forget it,' I say and go out, wanting sun, a long shadow reaching to me in the shadowless hut, but Douglas follows me, taking my arm, and I shake off his hand, but with something of fear rather than the rage that it seems.

'I'm sorry, Tom,' he is pleading with an abjectness that shames, and I am as shocked as I am discomforted to see that his lips are quivering and his eyes are struggling against tears. 'I *don't* like your idea and I wish you would see it my way, but I didn't have to be quite that catty back there.'

'I'll survive,' I say, trying for humour, which is hard because the 'catty' is as unsettling as 'wonderboy' – or am I loading these words with connotations that exist only in my own mind?

Desperately now I want to get away, extricate myself from the mire of my own puddling, but Douglas has that orderliness of mind that does not tolerate loose ends. 'You said I must forget it. Do you mean you agree now that I was right, that the subject is closed?'

'For now,' I dodge around the trap. 'Surely you don't expect me to see further than that? These are lying times, mate. Any morning we can wake up to a different fence. Even to a different Douglas and Tom. Who can say?' which could be cruel, but is also a *try* for honesty on my part, and I am hoping that the philosophical fuzziness of what I have said will bamboozle Douglas a shade, but I have my doubts as his eyes follow my walking away from what sounds like a silence of discontent.

I go straight across to Danny's hut – where else? – thinking, 'Christ! all this drama now and tomorrow that other drama when the curtain goes up,' that is if six stitched-together blankets can be called that, and grapple with a fresh pang of the stage fright that has been growing in me like a foetus all week.

'You walked in somebody's shit?' Danny asks as I slump down beside him on his bunk and he looks up from spooning out a tin of Red Cross Spam that he must have bought from his small stock of cigarettes, which unpremeditated spectacle seriously aggravates my mood.

'You should mash that into the swill,' I almost re-buke, forgetting that he's a one-man show and the dixie couldn't take it all, which imbalance he at once points out and I am abashed.

'You didn't answer my question,' he reminds and I say, Ja, it is something like that, and he wants to know more and I prevaricate, telling him only about tomor-row night and the stage fright, and he says I'll be all right, but offhandedly, as though he couldn't care all that much either way.

'Are you coming to the show?' I ask, not really sure whether I want him to say 'Yes' or 'No'.

'Nah. I like films. Cowboys, gangsters, that kind of stuff. My mum and the wife say that's for kids, but I don't care. A man likes what he likes and, to me, stage shows are just goons playing games that don't make me *believe*.'

I don't stay as long as I had planned, leave with the unwelcome feeling that although I earlier *almost* – how that sticks in my throat! – battled for Danny, this after-noon we seem a little further from each other than be-fore. Is it perhaps still because of the play and my association through it with Tony and the queer elements of the theatre world as a whole? Or is it because I have not dared to share the no holds barred tanning sessions with him, but have had to crouch in uneasy communica-tion in the hip-high space that the bunks allow?

Whatever the case, and although I return to Douglas' customary self, it has been, for me more than for most, a not very satisfying day, and I heave and groan under the swarming of the bugs and the as-harassing dreams of failure in the play, and in the morning and at lunch, and almost to the last moment before I robot out, Douglas begs me to eat, predicts my catastrophic collapse if I don't, but I don't, save for one small bread roll and a gutful of sugarless tea.

At the theatre, the staff are setting out whatever seating there is, which is not much, tardy patrons having to stand. Shouts, whistles, snatches of song – the staff get double rations and it shows – clatter and slap of boots, benches, chairs, echo under the high roof like a parallel other world, and I stare out over what is still so rawly only a shed and quail at the thought of the full house of four hundred pairs of sceptical eyes before which, soon now, we are to evoke an illusion as unlikely as the descent of a heavenly host. That the house *will* be full is hardly to be doubted because opening night is, as I told Danny, for the Ite brass, as also for the friends of the staff and cast (which means Douglas will be fussing over me any minute now if I don't haul arse), and any still empty seats or standing space will be quickly snapped up by the curious not so few who can't wait for their hut to take its turn at the subsequent shows, but must even now bay for the blood of Tom Smith's me 'playing games'.

'Come, Tom, let's do you now,' and Tony is beside me, talking quietly as to a condemned man, and I follow him to the barber's chair behind the stage and sit in it as though it were quite some other chair, and he looks at me as at a piece of meat and sets to work turning me into what, I am sure, I am never going to be inside.

'You're scared,' he states, does not ask, and I nod.

'I'm going to shit myself. Right there on stage.'

He laughs, gently, as one dealing with the insane. 'No, don't do that. Vomit before you go on, if that is what you feel you must do. That I won't mind because an actor who walks out there like it isn't the Last Day, is not and never will be worth a damn.' Then suddenly, passionately, 'I'm depending on you, kid. You're not the lead, but you have the lines by which the play stands or falls. I'm not forgetting it's your first time and how first-timers always feel. Like, for instance, you looking at that lot there,' and he jerks his head at the rest of the cast who have already been 'done' and are now slouching around as though this was just another boring chore, 'and thinking you're way down in the scale from ape to man. Forget them, kid. They are just a bunch of bloody queens like me who know I know why they're here, but I had to take them, partly because they are all there is and partly because they are, at least, experienced enough and sassy enough to hold the show on the road. But they are not the ones who will make this thing more than a fairy tale with moves. That, as I said, *you* have to do for me.'

'But why did you pick on *me*?' I ask and flinch at my voice's coming out like a cawing crow's.

He grins his more familiar savage grin. 'Because you are the meat that fits the bill. You *look* like that still fresh-faced more-lamb-than sheep that's wandered from the no longer so green fields of England into the shit that is the Somme. What is more, you don't even have to *try* for his awkwardness of the boy amongst the men.

Just say your lines the way I taught you and the peasants will be eating out of your hand.'

'Like I have out of yours?' I hit back, a quick bitterness curing the caw. 'Is that the way you have always seen me? Just another gormless pommy clown?'

'Come now, you know that is not true,' and he pinches my cheek with a vicious twist of his finger and thumb.

Freed, I sit on the box for the prompt in a corner of the stage and twitch the curtain aside. The camp band arrives with a ringing clangour of brass and hollownesses of drums, and goes to the back of the stage where it will have fun making like war while flashing lights simulate bursting shells. Most of the seats already host their bums and I see Douglas is in his, right behind the still vacant row for the Ites, and he is laughing and chattering to the total strangers about him as though he has known them a million years. It is, I am feeling, like watching the countdown to the guillotine, and I am about to break and run when there is a sound like wind or waves, and I look out again and the now packed auditorium is rising as the camp commandant struts in with his as glittering boots-and-buttons brigade, faces fugitive under the seemingly never-the-right-size-caps and an aura about them of vino, cognac and pomade that I am swearing I am smelling all the way from here. Then the overhead lights are dimming into darkness until only the footlights still illumine the Ites, and Tony is saying, 'To the wings!' in a low but urgent voice, and the prompt is diving for his box, script in hand, and Tony is going down to his seat in the auditorium, and the curtain is cranking up even as we rustle like the cockroaches in the huts into the darkened sides of the stage.

Now at last alone, beyond help or flight, I try to kick-start myself out of the paralysis of my fear by remembering Tony's final words, but it is his stressing of the importance of my role that most clearly returns, and the weight of that, far from challenging me, sinks me like a stone. Is there, indeed, no way out? For a feverish moment I really do consider flight, but the suck of the blood is too fierce and the lot of the outcast too dire, and I am back to poising like a sprinter for the starter-gun of my cue.

I am also back to chasing after shreds of dialogue I am thinking I have forgotten – a practice, this, which Tony warned us could affect the spontaneity of our lines – and I am still doing that when my cue sounds and I am on stage as suddenly and involuntarily as though a hand had shoved me there, and I commit the ultimate offence of glancing aside into Tony's furious frown, and the single, silent breath of the audience is coming at me over the footlights as though I had, after all, decided to cut and run.

My recall of my lines proves to be total, but the damage is done. I am a robot reporting for duty in a stage setting of a dugout that is a small masterpiece of innovation, but to me is no more than a painted mishmash of hardboard and cardboard making like wood. I am Thomas Aloysius Smythe, sometimes known as Tom Smith, and I am that and nothing more as my scene ends and I quit the stage, not daring to again glance aside, but sensing, none the less, that Tony is sitting there, his head bowed and his eyes closed.

Unnerved, telling myself I do not care, yet most deeply caring, I wait for my second entrance and it comes and I have blessedly nothing to say while the other officers talk about home, family, friends, the lone-liness of war. Then I move to the front of the stage, fac-ing out over the audience, and the always half-cut captain asks me if the cat has my tongue, and I am gath-ering up what little is left of me before I launch into the long monologue that is a pivotal part of the play, when I look down and see that three of the Ite officers have quit their seats on the left-hand end of their row and Danny, with the audaciousness that is Danny, is sitting in one of them and watching me with not-saying eyes.

Neither encouragement nor challenge passes from him to me, yet suddenly, joyously, I am challenged and, as suddenly, I am no longer Tom Smith, but the home-sick hardly more than a boy telling how it is against a background of phoney shells and candles guttering in as phoney a dugout turned real. Tony's face lifts to me in a blaze of interest, but I am talking, primarily, to Danny and, through him, to every other listening heart, and I know they *are* listening because their stillness tells me so, and I know Danny is listening because his eyes are no longer watching people playing games.

The play ends with me lying dying in what is left of the dugout when a shell hits it, which means I get to speak the last few lines, which is great but also no easy ride because I have to deliver in a whisper that must be heard by every ear in the house. I lost count of how many times Tony shouted, 'Jesus Christ!' when, in rehearsal, I could not get it right, but now I'm *going* to get it right because the persona is about me like a second skin – I was going to say like an FL round a wally, but now is hardly the time – and there is a great gnashing of instruments by the band at the back of the stage, and Tony's stagehands let slip the set's staying ropes and the whole painted trickery is sliding down over me, and my whisper is ghosting out, as effortless as it is clear, and the drummer, inspired, is dropping a single beat between the lines.

'Have I served like an officer and a man?' I am asking as the lights go up and the curtain sags down, and Tom Smith, taking back what is his, is thinking, 'Pure fucking corn!' but the audience has swallowed it, turds and all, and though I cannot say there is a standing ovation because half the audience has been standing anyway, the clapping goes on long enough and the Ites are doing their bit like the good guys I suddenly think they are. Then we are lining up in front of the curtain and Tony is pumping hands and slapping backs and bounding around like a satyr chasing nymphs – or whatever it is queer satyrs chase – and the commandant is also doing his duty round, but sharing with me a sharp glance as well as his hand, and I am seeing that the hated face is basically an old man's with tired eyes and maybe there is a buxom wife with bambinos somewhere far away who is binding him to us with a measure of common pain.

Again Danny is brashly he, not waiting for us to

leave the stage, but coming down the line to only me, proffering first a distancing hand, then briefly, determinedly embracing me, saying, '*Better* than any film, mate,' and I sense that he is making a move of sorts in a game that has barely begun.

'Who was that cocky little chap who went up and' – is there a hesitancy before the word? – 'hugged you after the show?' Douglas asks when we are back in the hut. 'Isn't it the one who was tanning alongside you a few days ago?'

'Could be,' I casually carefully say, wondering what is to come.

'Why only "could be"? Don't you *know*?'

'After a show like that, Douglas, I hardly know who *I* still am. Try it and see.'

'Poor man,' he at once concedes. 'Let me make us some tea.' And we drink our tea and everything seems fine, but, now and again, glancing at him unexpectedly, I trap a speculativeness in his eyes that I have not before seen and almost I again hear the drummer dropping those single beats between my lines.

————⟶✦⟵————

It is on a night some weeks after the show has completed its run, that Danny makes his second unmistakably intrusive move.

During the day, it being a Monday, Douglas and I slog our way through the week's accumulation of laundry handed to us at sparrow-fart by our still sleepily grumbling dice-and-poker kings. At such a penitent's hour, we are no less fretful, but it is necessary to be amongst the first three of the score or so laundrymen that each Monday bolt with gritting teeth down to the ablution block with its matching only three waist-high scrubbing slabs. The alternative is to spend a day of backbreaking gymnastics at the more general purpose taps and the struggle for turf is often as pitiless as the drive for the top of the heap of the mini-mobsters we serve. Douglas, however, loves the challenge, rises to it as though it is some bizarre new sport, and, in the process, has developed an awesome capacity for anticipating our rivals' awakenings, jolting me out of sleep at the oddest moments as his antennae warn him of a blanket sliding from cunning flesh.

So we rarely lose out on the slabs and we happily do not lose out today, but that is about the only cause for jubilation because our customers, like the benevolent godfathers that they are not, seem to have decided that we need to earn more 'cash' now that the Red Cross food deliveries are becoming ever more irregular for a reason that the Ites are choosing to not disclose. Thus, the week's wash has never been bulkier and this is, indeed, welcome because it *will* earn us more, but the apparent charitableness is offset by the fact that the wash has also never been filthier, the man-size handkerchiefs, in particular, crackling with dried mucus that reverts back to slime when wetted and clings to the linen like a hibernating snail.

Handkerchiefs? Here? Why not? The stalls may be selling only foodstuffs but there are also occasional markets that start up with the suddenness of dust devils and, like them, whirl out amongst the huts, growing as they go into a milling mass of shouting touters that cause new guards to fiddle with their rifle-bolts and call out to the long-suffering Virgin for her aid. There is no buying and selling in the conventional sense of such words, rather a swapping of an article for an article, the unwanted for the wanted, and the transactions vary from the relatively major blanket for a coat to the humble handkerchief's enticing as humble a sock.

Not everybody there is a swapper, though. Many, myself and Douglas included, go there for the one commodity that is for the taking, namely, the reverse of the tedium that is the very essence – and curse – of our purposeless lives. Now and again, we may go hunting for soap – not the latherless Ite soap that smells like a whore and bites like a snake that our mafia clients get for us from the guards, then deduct the price from our fee, but that genuine *soap* that, like so much that was once commonplace, now glows with the luminance of myth or dream.

Like the Ite soap which is the most necessary element of it, the laundering process is very far removed from myth and dream. It is, instead, one of those ultimately harsh and demeaning realities from which, had it not been for Douglas' pacing me with his clinical attitude of the male nurse, I would long since have fled. My hands no longer blister from the scrubbing, but, at day's end, their skin is pallid and puffy as that of a waterlogged corpse, and I keep smelling my fingers as though I expect to find on them the lingering miasmas of all the snot, shit and even sperm that they have wrung – as though they wrung the neck of loathesomeness itself – from the most intimate garments of those from whom I could not be more estranged. Or have I, through such handling of their pitiful effluents, subtly and irreversibly grown closer to them than even the most passionate of lovers could?

But there is more. Mondays, if we have won the race for the slabs, as today we did, we have to arrange with the hut boss for him to fetch our midday swill and hold it in the hut till we return, there being no question of our leaving our slab for anything more than a quick piss, let alone to have a leisurely lunch or brew ourselves a mug of tea. To do so would be to find ourselves deprived of our slab with no hope of its return, that being the law of the camp and the name of the game, besides which the washing must be hung, dried, folded and delivered before sunset, there being no space in the huts for working with washing and any attempt to retrieve washing still on the fences after dark liable to be construed as a break-out and met by a bullet in the brain. Even the hanging of washing on the fences in daylight caused the commandant to, at first, squeal like a slaughterhouse hog, but, eventually, we wore him down.

So the upshot of it all is that, this Monday, the last foldings of laundry delivered, Douglas and I return to the hut to count the day's takings and eat lunchtime's hardening shit with a relish that is nought on a scale of that to ten, and we consider brewing tea to wash down the accompanying rolls, but tiredly decide to drink water instead, and, from my bunk, I watch Douglas readying himself for sleep and there is a resurgence in me of liking and respect whose very fullness illustrates how severe the ebbing had lately become. Then the Ites

cut the old-bone yellow of the lights and Douglas sets
out on his litany of prayers, but I plunge straight away
into sleep, still fully clothed and, for once, oblivious of
the bugs.

And it seems as though I had only just closed my
eyes, when someone is calling my name, and I start up
as from a dream, but it is no dream, but Danny standing in the doorway of the hut and crying out in a low
yet carrying voice, 'Tom! Wake up! Wake up!' and I am
out and hurrying, driven not only by the urgency of his
tone but by the fact that this is the first time that
Danny has ever come to our hut – a strangeness, this,
which he and I have never discussed, tacitly agreeing
that to do so would be to precipitate a crisis in a three-
way relationship which none of us was as yet prepared
to confront. Or was *he* now so prepared?

Descending from my bunk, I see that Douglas is
still asleep in his, but the rest of the bunks – even the
interloper's – seem empty and there is a hollowness to
the hut as a whole that smacks of abandonment in the
face of some peril of a fearsome shape. I reach the door
and Danny seizes my arm, almost dragging me out, and
I am about to irritably break free, when I see that a
host of thousands of us are standing between the huts,
motionlessly and silently as though bewitched, faces up-
turned under the full moon to the flank of the nearby
hill, eyes staring as before the advent of a presence of a
celestial kind.

'What is it?' I instinctively whisper, but Danny does
not answer, only grips my arm the harder, secretively
smiles.

Then it again sounds and my hairs are hackles and my flesh crawls.

'A nightingale,' Danny now whispers back, hand not loosing my arm. 'Bet you never heard one before. Even in Blighty you don't hear them so much any more.'

But I am barely aware of him now, hear only 'nightingale', am of these spellbound under the witches' moon. 'So small a throat!' I am thinking. '*So small a throat!*' as the soaring gusts of sound, pitched a note's breadth this side of sense, flood, copiously as the moon's light, effortlessly as that which needs no struggling breath nor fiddling hand, out over hills, churches, shrines, our ragbag selves. There is no pattern to the song, yet it holds the whole of melody and the totality of an endlessness of form, and it runs a thread of molten yet cool-aswater silver through my every artery, sinew, vein, and I search for a humanness in it, but there is nothing, and now I am thinking, 'An *angel*! Strayed from Eden's gates without its sword!' and for a moment I am near again to the child that so easily believed.

'Douglas must hear this, too,' I say and make to go, caution overturned, meanness yielding its ground in the face of that pure sound.

But he does not loose my arm. 'I came to wake *you*, not *him*,' he says, his voice challenging and cold, and I stand, irresolute, a choosing come upon me that I had not planned.

'Anyway,' he adds, 'he's already awake,' and he jerks his head and I see Douglas is standing a few paces to the right of us, his own head turning even as I turn

mine and the three of us playing one of those seemingly
silly games with a sting in the tail, Russian roulette
being *the* one.

Covertly, I try to glean from Douglas' profile
whether he has, indeed, seen us and, if so, what his reaction is likely to be, but he is now staring steadfastly and
apparently raptly at the hill, and continues to do so
until the singing again stops and there is an almost
audible draining of earth and sky – and an almost tangi-
ble quality to the ensuing void – that tell us that the
bird has flown, and Douglas turns, quietly but decisively, and goes back into the hut without once glancing
our way, and it is only then that I notice that Danny is
no longer holding my arm.

'Ah, young Tom,' says Camel as though the earth beside me had opened to let him out. Then, belatedly,
'And friend. But why so pensive? It was only a bird,
you know.'

'All the more reason to be humble, Camel,' I lash
back, nerves frayed, and he winces, getting what I
mean.

'Subtle, young Tom. But not nice. Nor you. Are we
not, then, still friends?'

I decide it is to be peace, not war. 'Come *on*,
Camel. I thought you knew me by now.'

'Oh, I do. I do. Though not in the way I would prefer.' Then, looking at Danny but addressing me, 'Did
you ever pass on my message to your friend?'

I'm cornered and know it, so can but bluster as best
I know how. 'Christ, no. What with the play being on
and the Red Cross not coming through like it should,

it's as if I've been in another world. But, in any case, you haven't finished doing me yet, so why do you want him as well?'

'But I *have* finished you. Only I'm not giving you what I have done. Do you expect me to after all the shitty things you had to say? And what makes you think I can't do more than one painting at a time? I have got two hands, haven't I?' and he gives his little cackle that sounds like dry leaves blowing over sand.

'Who's this goon?' Danny chips in, his tone warning me that another crisis is heading my way. 'And what's the gab about a message I didn't get?'

'This,' and I try to keep my voice casual, though a quake is beginning in me somewhere deep down, 'is Camel. He paints. Portraits, not walls. Those who are supposed to know about these things say he has got class. *I* wouldn't know. All I know is that he's done a picture of me and I look like a steak that's looking for an eye. He says that's because he paints people without their skins. Paints them the way they really *are*, not the way they *think* they are. So,' and I breathe deep before I leap, 'just before the play, he asked me to tell you that he wants to paint you too.'

'So? Why didn't you tell me, then?'

My mind scuttles round like a rat in a cellar with the door closed. 'Because I was sure he would make as big a mess of you as he did of me.'

'Not quite true, young Tom,' Camel chides. 'Are you and Douglas still sharing the chow?' and it takes me far too long to work out what this apparent non sequitur means.

But Danny again breaks in, turning to Camel for the first time, a tautness to him that evokes an equal tautness in me. 'So how, then, would you be seeing *me* if I said OK?'

And Camel laughs his rustling, dry laugh and I am thinking he may or may not be a good painter, but he most certainly is going to be one helluva fool. 'Naked!' he crows, clearly remembering that 'goon', raddled eyes alight with perceptiveness and the laugh a meaningless noise. 'Naked and playing with your prissy little balls.'

There is also no doubt that Danny is every bit as good a boxer as he claims. Now Camel is still standing, not grinning with his slash of a mouth, then he is crashing back against the side of our hut, mouth chewing on a rose of his blood, and probably a tooth or two, and some from the hut, Douglas not among them, are cluttering up the step and wondering what the fuck is going on.

Fists raised, Danny waits for Camel to get up so that he can give him another go, but Camel, quick to learn now that it is too late, stays where he is, and Danny turns to me, his face inward as a stone. 'I made a mistake,' he says, his voice matching his face. 'If this is the kind of friends you keep, then you are not one of mine,' and goes.

A gravity of misery settles in me, anchoring me to where I stand, then one of my flashy rages seizes me and I yell, 'Who said I was one of your friends, anyway?' and turn back to Camel, not knowing whether I am going to help him up or let him lie.

But he is already up, swaying a little, spitting out blood, reaching for my arm. 'Christ, Tom,' he mumbles through the ruin of his mouth. 'I'm sorry, man. So *sorry*. I never meant it to be like this.'

'Fuck off,' I mumble back, wrenching loose, but there is no spirit in that and I go into the hut, dragging my misery with me like a busted leg.

Sitting on his bunk, Douglas is watching his hands as though they might at any moment cut and run. But I take no notice of him, only struggle my way up onto my own bunk and flop down on it, face to the light, arm over my eyes.

But Douglas is not one to leave well alone. 'Why didn't you wake me?' he asks in a voice as distant as the wrong side of the moon.

'Don't *you* start now!' I seethe and turn onto my side, spine to the aisle.

'I'm not starting anything,' he persists. 'I'm just asking why you didn't wake me up?'

'Why should I have woken you up when I didn't know what was going on till I got outside?'

'Well, why didn't you wake me up *then*?'

'You *heard*, didn't you?' I say, and need to say no more because, despite my deviousness and distress, there is a resurgence in me, as in my voice, of the just past wonderment and awe.

Then I wait for him to ask the really awkward questions, but he skirts around them as though they were a poisoned bait, and later, when everyone is asleep, I go out and sit on the step, waiting for the bird to sing again, though knowing with a knowing that is not of the mind that silence is all I am going to hear.

I am thinking that it is Danny who said something that meant, 'Take away the Red Cross cigarette and our economy is dead.' As then, inevitably, we also will be.

I am remembering this – while I am trying to not re-member *him* – because this is no longer a postulate but a fact. The deliveries of Red Cross cigarettes and food have become so erratic and scarce that starvation is a spectre no further than my neighbour's face and his breath is the corruption that is death's. The stalls run out of stocks, which means the cigarette's buying power nose-dives and you might as well smoke it yourself and so anaesthetize your mind into believing that you are not as hungry as you are. So not only the stalls close down, but the gambling kings, most of whom are heavy smokers, choose to smoke rather than gamble and the laundrymen like Douglas and me no longer have a trade. The gamblers embarrassedly start washing their own underpants, and Douglas and I, neither of us being smokers, stash away whatever cigarettes we still have in the hope that they will still be of use someday, then join the noonday swill queue with increasingly the same avidity as the common herd. The great leveller that is indigence is amongst us and the only truly class-less society begins to grow independently of our voli-tion as a cancer or age.

We crack the irreverent jokes of the cast-out and the condemned, only they are not jokes – more like little kids' shouting at the bogeyman in the hope that that will make him go away. Each day there are events of minor horror that we know will stay with us longer than slaughter for the very reason that they *are* so minor, even hilarious, like when our hut boss, weak with incipient dysentery, sits too long on one of the seats over the shit pit and a rat, from those swarming down there, jumps up and bites him in the balls. For days afterwards, we howl with laughter about that; or about the one of us with the usually outsized eyes that now have grown huge, who looks over the edge of his bunk and despairingly gapes, but only contrives to look more like a nestling waiting to be fed a worm; or about the no longer portly and pontificating ex-magistrate who, for hours on end, will sit on his bunk with his trademark tiny wooden spoon and scoop out margarine that is no longer there from an old Red Cross margarine can, then smack his lips with a relish that is ghoulishly unfeigned.

But there is a wildness to the howling, a whimpering in its ebbing, that have nothing to do with laughter and everything to do with the hollow-flanked beast with its red bat's-eyes that has become our familiar and follows us with the passion of a predator its prey. Camel, who each day prepares his easel and paints, then sits staring at them as though stricken by a curse, tells me that the beast has finally caught up with the one man in their hut who could still make them laugh on an empty gut.

'Real clown, he was,' he says. 'Should have been on the stage. Now he's stashed away in the Ites' loony bin.' I ask him what happened and he asks if I remember the lone tap beside the theatre where you can stop for a quick drink, and I nod and he says they caught him there, hiding round a corner of the theatre and shaking like a jelly because of the funniness of what, it turned out, he had been doing for a long time. 'He would take some shit from the shit pit,' Camel explains. 'How he got it from down there, don't ask me. Or maybe he just sat himself down anywhere and had a shit and used some of his own stuff. Whatever, he would then roll the shit into little balls and line them up behind the theatre so's he could keep popping them up the tap and watch while the drinkers took a suck at the tap like it's a titty and out comes the crap,' and he can't help snickering a little himself, but my flesh crawls.

Sometimes I go down to the theatre, but no one is interested in plays any more, and Tony is as listlessly idle as Camel and the old shed booms like a cavern of despair. I will touch the props or the band's still valiantly glittering brass, but the dust on my fingers is a weeping and the air whispers of irreclaimable dreams. Occasionally, Tony's eyes behind the pince-nez will light up with a ghost of the old enthusiasm and he will speak of London and its theatres before the war, but it is all only an exercise in nostalgia and soon there is a turning inwards again, and a switching-off of the light as after a show, and I know that it is time for me to go.

Douglas and I, of course, are the most graphic mirrors, each to the other, of how we change – the sharpening features, the eyes' remotenesses alternating with anxious immediacies, the sagging skins of belly and dugs, the hands now comatose, now breaking into the transient, frenzied life of leaves whipped by a gusting wind. There are also changes of *habit* that leave as telling a spoor – my innate untidiness' sliding into slovenliness, Douglas' still cleaning the dixies but no longer scouring them till they shine, and, most poignantly of all, his grown laboured reading with its long pauses for staring into nothing at all.

As I watch Douglas so change, what do I feel? Grief? Grief is a very *heavy* word. Regret, certainly, and a measure of pain. Pity, too, although that, with typical selfishness, is as much for me as for him. Perhaps I could have reacted more expansively had there not been other changes in him which have nothing whatever to do with hunger and merely irritate me in much the manner of the bugs, which have not ceased to feed on us though we must, by now, be proffering them a far from fortifying blood. That very next morning, at the latest, he must have heard about Danny's fight with Camel and the ensuing bust-up between Danny and me, which will explain why, ever since, he has treated me with a mixture of compassion and triumphalism that cannot but arouse in me an endemic if suppressed annoyance that seriously tempers any feelings of pity I may now be having for *him*.

Now that I have told myself that I am finished with Danny, that I never want to see him again, I seem destined to see him nearly every day – on the toilet, at the taps, startlingly rounding a corner as I kill time on my occasional slow prowlings round the camp. Should I happen – or so I put it to myself – to walk past the grass-patch with its warming sun, I will invariably see him lying there, though no longer where we used to lie with touching sides, and his body fully clothed as if he would conceal the shaming insurgencies of its bones. Emotion never fails to seize me then, shake me like a puppy a ball or doll, and I try to tell myself that it is anger that I feel, though I know it is pain, otherwise why is there in me such a clear relief that he has, seemingly, stopped his daily shambling round the fence and so spared me the turning away that anger surely should have reversed? Also, and more subtly, why should I then always be comparing that emotion, its intensity and intractability, with the lacklustre concern I have for Douglas' slide into the skeletal and, by so doing, realize anew that I am entrapped in a limbo whose name I am not yet ready to hear?

Sometimes I try to face up to the amorphous beast of how I feel, lend it shape, substance, of which I can ask questions, have hope of a reply. Already my mind, recalcitrant rebel that it is, has framed such unspeakable questions as, 'Am I one of *them*? Am I in love with a *man*?' But I beat these questions back with the desperateness of one under siege, then with a deliberate crudeness dwell on the mechanics of sex between males. 'Comes out all covered with shit!' I think and shudder with a quite genuine disgust, yet am none the less still uncomfortably aware that the question of love itself stays unresolved, is being linked by me to the sexual act in the simplistic and grubby-minded manner of adolescents in order that I may frighten myself back into the cosy straitjacket into which I was born and raised. From there it is an easy step to the usual acrimonious diversions, such as, 'Who does the little fart think he is, anyway?' and, 'Fuck him! Why should I worry about a fucking pom?' But, again, there is no real anger in me – only a far echo of a child's longing for a taken-away toy.

But then there is a diversion of quite another kind as the long fuse of the hungry and powerless at last flares to its end and ignites us into rising up in a cause that has a far from lofty aim. Or is loftiness as frailly relative as are space and time? Whatever, the hut bosses put out the word that we are all to gather at the main gate at the next day's dawn, then start marching in ranks of ten, arms linked, round and round the fence, demanding that our huts be debugged and vowing to not stop, no matter what, until the Ites have agreed to our demand. Which is not as crazy as it sounds because the Ites have a very real dread of inspections by Red Cross officials – thus carefully papering over all cracks before each visit – and a mass murder of legitimately protesting prisoners is hardly the scenario they would choose. But we are more than a little jittery, all the same, and lie awake till late, chirruping like bats and alternating between bravado and fear.

In the morning, the still half-asleep guards do not at first grasp what is going on as we noiselessly muster, then begin to march with a sudden challenging roar that we had not guessed we still had the breath to sustain. Then the guards are very much awake, lancing us with searchlights from the raised-up sentry boxes and, on the ground, scampering beside us, fence between, in a ludicrous parallel march that would make us laugh were we not so shit-scared inside. But our nerves steady as we sense that the Ites' shrieks are tinged with as much of our fear as their rage, and we grow positively cocky as the bullets continue to whine well clear of our heads and we see the commandant is coming out, still

buttoning his tunic as he mounts the steps to a sentry
box, loud-hailer in his hand.

He bellows for silence, and the hut bosses signal for
that, so we give him silence, and he rages on and on, rising onto his toes, sinking back onto his heels, huffing
himself up like a pigeon with the hots, clawing at the
heavens with quivering hands. Then he passes the loud-
hailer to the interpreter siding him, clumps down from
the box, struts back to the barracks, buttocks jiggling
like a whore's, and the interpreter, in a single sentence
of staccato but otherwise impeccable English, tells us
that the commandant has agreed to our request – carefully he sidesteps 'demand' – and will we now fuck off
back to our huts before he changes his mind? The sun
is now well up and we wilt, the adrenalin, that we had
thought to be energy, gone as though it had never been,
and, in us, a hollowness as though a cosmic breath had
sucked the very marrow from our bones, and we begin
to dawdle our way back to the huts and the torpor that
infests them with a malevolence that even the bugs cannot match.

They are upon us before we can run, shield, rebuff.
Clubbing at us with their rifle-butts, yelling as though
the once wild hills had resurrected their barbarous
hordes, the Ite guards are clearly out to reassert their
hold over us, beat us back into the necessary submissiveness and fear, which, strangely enough, I can understand, although that does not help me any as a rifle-butt
crashes into the side of my head and a carnival of lights
explodes in my brain.

Looking up at the bow legs straddling me, I see that

they belong to a more than usually runty Ite whose face is neither brutish nor innocent, merely peasant and dull, and, above the stolid set of the lips, is a thin smudge of a moustache that suggests that he has a way with women and devotes himself to that with a simple passion that could have endeared him to me at some other time and in some other place. I also notice that there is a dark stain in the crotch of his blue-grey uniform's pants that could be a sweat of the fear that he is wishing for me, and there is a pathos to that that still does not dissuade me from wanting to grab at and crush his testicles with all the strength of the enemy that I am, but my head is spinning as if the threads of the anchoring neck have stripped and I close my eyes and steel myself for the butt's follow-up blow.

But then Douglas is yelling at him with a sassiness that is strange, that reaches to me through the swaddling pain, and the Ite, as strangely, leaves us alone, and Douglas is helping me to my feet and steadying me with a mothering hand. 'You poor man!' he is saying, a phrase, this, which he has used before and which I loathe as much now as I did then, but, after what he has done, I am not so boorish as to let it show and even let him drape my arm about his neck so that he can more easily half-drag me along. And it is then that I look up and Danny is standing in the doorway of his hut and watching us pass with eyes that say he is as disinterested in my bludgeoned and blundering state as he would be in a stray dog struck down by a car, and, at last, the true anger for which I have been searching possesses me and I stare back at him with a hatred no words can hold, and would know a catharsis, then, were it not for a slyness in me that asks, 'Why so *violent* a hate if nothing is there?'

————⠀————

For once, the Ites are true to their word, although they do not keep it without some measure of their usual spite, ordering us out of the huts before dawn in order, no doubt, to pay us back for *our* dawn disruption of the previous day, then making us stand around in the sun till it sets while they debug the huts with the minimum of energy they are prepared to expend. But, at least, it gets *done* and, in a further placatory move, the commandant produces a full round of Red Cross food parcels from the fuck alone knows where, and we go into festive overdrive about this even though it strengthens a long-standing rumour that the Ites are sitting on a mountain of parcels and slowly white-anting them away.

We deal with this unexpected and, probably, one-off distribution in one of two ways — consume it lingeringly over as many days as your lust can stand, or follow the ex-magistrate who also consumes his slowly but all at once in a binge that lasts nightlong, then vomits it out again and knows neither regret nor shame. For the overwhelming majority of us, the latter course is little short of blasphemy, while the former can best be likened to an erection's gradual and agonizingly delicious inching into the final thrust and flurry that are, then, all the more abandoned for having been reined in for so long. Douglas is rather proud of the way he and I manage and thinks it wonderful that the camp should so soon again be sitting up and taking nourishment, and I

99

am thinking he has a point there – Camel again reaching for his pencil, eyes quickening with visions of genitals, and Tony fantasising about another show – but then I'm changing my mind and I say, 'Nah! Why wonderful? All it's saying is that there is no spirit without the meat. Starve the belly and that's all we are – meat wanting more meat so that it can *go on* being meat!' and Douglas says I am cynical and I know that he is right while I am wishing that he was wrong.

So life is back like the last faint flush summoned by a dying face, sleep is deep in the bugless huts and I am again eating from a dixie that shines from Douglas' scrubbing it with sand. Convinced now that nothing better is coming my way and far too introverted to go out and search for anything other from my side, I reattune myself to my relationship with Douglas, arguing that although it may be about as exhilarating as warmed-over swill, there *are* certain creature comforts attached to it and *any* relationship is better than, say, our interloper's drifting in his limbo for the alone.

Then, of a sudden, wrenching us out of our easygoing flowing with the stream, the old rumour of lice is up and running again, and we are conscious that there is still an itchiness to us though the bugs are gone, and there is a camp-wide furtive checking on crotches and a finding of the telltale nits and even the odd pallid adult's insolent clambering over the pubic hairs.

Needless to say, Douglas, male nurse dixie-scrubber that he is, howls the loudest at this ultimate subversion of his personal hygiene. 'Shit!' he babbles, almost weeping. 'I am *infested*!' and, despite my own condition, I

am more than a little pitilessly amused that it should
have taken a louse to provoke him into the first gritty
word I have yet heard him use.

The tussle over the bedbugs has taught us that suffering in silence is not the way to go, so the hut bosses
haul arse to see our go-between and he comes back to
them and says the Ites are expecting an inspection by
high-ranking Red Cross officials, which is why they
gave in so easily about the bedbugs, and they are nip-
ping straws now that he's told them about the lice and
threatened that the camp will be marching again. But it
never comes to that because, the next morning, the Ites'
croupy bugle is summoning us to a mustering of the
huts on the open ground in front of the main gates, and
the Ites are fanning out amongst us and we are dropping our pants like it's a short arm inspection in the
forgotten times.

Culled and counted, it turns out that only several
hundred of us are actually 'unclean' – Douglas' word,
not mine – and these mostly from the huts in the immediate vicinity of the pommy hut – does the hare of my
rage flare its ears? – which is the most heavily infested,
this leading to a pointing of fingers that promises we
are to be a far from happy band. Clearly, there has been
an infestation more of the minds than of the groins, but
the Ites (give them their due) are determined to do a
good job with what they have, and we are told to fetch
the rest of our clothes from our huts and report back,
when we are marched out of the camp and into a grassy
paddock at the back of the barracks where devil-eyed
goats stare at us with the malevolence of their kind.

'Strip,' says what appears to be a medical orderly who speaks a little English helped by eloquent hands, and we strip, some lightheartedly, some grimly and a few, like Douglas, primly, and the Ites gather up our clothes, both the just shed and the spare, and pile them onto pushcarts and trundle them across to the hospital which looks more like a factory with its cracked and dust-laden panes and annexe with a stack where, presumably, the clothes will be deloused. Ten pairs of scissors are handed out at random and we are told to snip short our pubic hairs, which takes the usual trillion years, then our shorn crotches are puffed full of a white powder which could be cake flour or quicklime for all we know, and we are ordered into yet another queue, this time for the chow that we missed at noon, only it is not swill, our dixies still being in the huts, but a double ration of rolls and a chunk of the Ite cheese that is to die for and that we haven't seen since I don't know when.

There are taps outside the infirmary, so we wash the rolls down with water from there, and nobody is worrying about us much because although to make a break with a naked snake is possible, this is not the age of runaway satyrs and the Ites would not have much difficulty following our scandalizing spoor. By now, the sun is low and we are getting goose skin from the first chill, and although we try not to look at each other too openly, a sidelong glance at a sudden flurry of activity on the part of Douglas tells me that he has produced a handkerchief – from a hand held clenched all this while? – and is trussing up his penis and balls, which should be funny enough to make me piss myself, but which only boundlessly embitters me that I should have such an old aunty for a mate.

Relentlessly, the sun slips lower, seems to flutter a moment on the spine of the hill, is gone, and the goats start to bed down, still watching us with mingled curiosity and mistrust, and we start to shout for our clothes, but the Ites make us form another queue instead and begin to dish out blankets, one for every two men, and it becomes plain that we are to spend the night among the goats, and I think of all those snipped-off pubic hairs with their nits and the crawling crabs of their lice that I imagine we are trampling on, will maybe be sleeping on, and my stomach heaves and, for a moment, I am no better than Aunty Douglas with her bandaged-up balls.

Douglas it is that says he will fetch our blanket and I can stand guard over the place in the shortest of the goat-cropped grass – I insisting on that – where we have decided to kip, and I say, 'OK,' and he goes and I stand watching the first stars check in and thinking of that city beside the sea where the wanker is maybe still grappling with the demon in his loins.

'You want to share my blanket?' he asks and I turn and he is standing a pace away, a blanket over his arm.

My first impulse is to turn away again and my tongue gropes to shout, 'Fuck off!' but his eyes stay me, though they neither coerce nor invite, merely wait without any particular expectancy for me to say either 'Yes' or 'No', and there is a great rushing between us as of a wind's passing, though nothing stirs. Frantically I reach out to Douglas, seeking an anchorage in his frustrating faithfulness, seeking it in even his foibles that aggravate me most, but I am standing in a bright water of wanting that is washing away the sand beneath me as though it, too, is a water that will not be denied.

'Wait here,' I hear myself say, my voice distant and rustling as that sea's reaching for the city in an irretrievable time, and I go up the queue to where Douglas is standing and, with a last of decency left in me, do that which is as cowardly as it is brave.

'Listen,' I whisper, 'there's a personal matter I have to settle with a guy who's here now. So I'll be sharing a blanket with him tonight to thrash the thing out. See you tomorrow at the hut,' and I grip his shoulder in a show of intimacy that shames but does not make me break step in my drive for what I want, and I hear Douglas draw in his breath as though he feels a blade slide into his side.

Danny is still standing where I left him, a solidness to the standing as of one who belongs, his eyes aware of my decision and distress as though I had spoken aloud, and he jerks his head and I follow him to a place as far removed as we can find from where Douglas and I would have slept. Not speaking, we sit down, then lie back, faces to the now full night, and he throws the blanket over us and I tuck it in on my side and he on his, and the silence goes on till, without turning my head, I ask, 'Why?'

He does not ask, 'Why what?' or play games, at once replies, 'I'm trusting your hands. I told you how I am.'

*That* I did not expect. What *did* I expect? A profession of undying friendship, of contrition for stalking off into the night or watching me being beaten up by the Ite? My knowledge of him tells me I'm a fool for even *thinking* that he would expose himself in such a way, but I'm disappointed all the same and cannot resist letting it show. 'Well, you proved to me how good you are with your fists, so why couldn't you just clobber anyone who tried to muck you around?'

'I'd sooner just sleep,' he says, his voice amused as though he's guessed what I'm really wanting from him, and turns onto his side, his back to me, his buttocks warmly against my thigh, and I check myself for the usual dislike of that, but there is nothing, and I think, then, of Douglas, wonder if some gritty pom was all that he could find, try to feel the low-down bum that I am. But it is hard now that there is so much of a repleteness in me, so much of a wholeness after a limping alone, and it is harder still when I think of how little I would have liked it had it been Douglas' buttocks that were warming my thigh.

As though aware of my warring selves, Danny starts to shake, startling me since I had thought he slept. Or *is* he sleeping and dreams? Uncertainly, I make to wake him, then see he is laughing and ask, 'What's the joke?' and he says, 'Us. Two blokes and all this time we are spiting each other like we're two bints!' and I know from the hollowness behind the laugh that that is the closest he is going to get to admitting he was a cunt.

Then, in quite a different tone, 'You chose tonight,' and I know with a fearful clarity what he means, but draw back from the final step, and he repeats, 'I said you chose tonight,' and now I take a half a step: 'Maybe,' I say, and he whirls around with the swiftness of an angered cat and his face almost touches mine and his eyes blaze. 'Don't give me that! You *did* choose! Between me and that twit with the handkerchief round his cock!'

'That's cruel.' How I sometimes can sound just like an old aunty myself, I think. Has so much of Douglas rubbed off onto me? 'We've wronged the poor guy enough as it is.'

'Cruel? What do you mean "cruel"? It's cruel that you're hitched up to a biddy like that. But now either you're my mate or you get your arse out of here and go back to whatever's his name.'

'*All right!*' I whisper-shout. 'So I am your mate, goddammit!'

'As though I would have let you go, anyway,' he grunts and turns back onto his side, settling down with a fussy shuffling of limbs.

'I hope you don't treat your wife this way,' I rebuke, hardly hiding how I really feel.

'She's not complaining,' and again the back shakes, and I punch it and it pretends to cringe and we sleep.

In what I sense is a sliding towards morning, I wake, aroused by the deepening cold. A moon, slumping into its crescent, is about to set behind the hill, its light brilliantly in my eyes, a dream slipping from me like water from a skin. A few paces off, an Ite is standing guard, his rifle's barrel jutting up behind him like an overgrown spine, his silhouette dark and motionless

as one of the paddock's posts, and, for a moment, I
am back in the desert, Douglas instead of Danny beside
me and the dawning of the second day of our shaming
only hours away. A goat bleats as though it, too, had
dreamt, but the sleepers about us are motionless as a
massacre, and, for the first time since our arrival in the
camp – the even midnight busyness of the huts no longer worrying my ears – I hear a train's wheels clicking
as it passes through the little station where, a year back,
they herded us from the trucks and we began the long
straggle up to the camp.

I can remember no lonelier sound, nor one that so
painfully proclaims the absoluteness of our banishment
from a world that each day slips further from us like
the dream's fleeing my brain; each day increasingly
seems the unreality and the myth and our bitter Eden
the only solid anchorage under the sun. Distressed, I
stir, struggle against the blanket's suddenly imprisoning
me, and Danny reverses sides, facing me now, but still
sleeping, an arm across my chest, his breath, faintly on
my cheek, smelling only of itself and his one knee resting on my thigh. He is bearing down on my arm that
lies straightly between us, palm upwards, and I try to
withdraw it, but the knee on my thigh slips over further, angling him more sharply towards me, and his
genitals flop down into my palm, the pubic hairs bristling against my wrist, but the penis and testicles slack
and warm as a plucked but still living bird.

Unlike the genitals, his body is cold, its saddening
boniness trembling slightly against my own rebellious
bones, and I lie, crucified on a crossroads of indecision

as to what to do. Should I push him away, thus surely waking him and reminding him of the day when I flinched from his finger's touching my cheek, or should I try to quietly withdraw my hand and arm and run the risk of his waking *then* and thinking – with fatal consequences – that I have just finished fondling his crotch? Interminable moments pass, a bird cries from the hill's slope, but it is no nightingale, and then irritation overtakes me – and a less predictable compassion for the vulnerable huddle in my palm – and I curve my fingers lightly over the core of his maleness with its waning warmth and think, 'To hell with it!' and sleep, his breath a trusting on my cheek.

When I again wake, the sun is up, but the air is still chill and the dew is heavy as a rain on the grass. Danny again has his back to me and could be asleep, except that there is about him a subtle stillness as of the watchfully awake, and I have this feeling that if I were to suddenly confront him, I would find his eyes sightless and staring as glass. Did he turn away from me in his sleep, thus releasing his genitals without his ever knowing where they had lain, or did he wake before that and find them entrapped in an unconsciously tightening hold? Anxiety mounts in me and I sit up with a deliberate abruptness, jiggling him, but he does not stir, and now I know that he *is* awake and his stillness is a sullenness, else why does he not speak or turn?

Sick with guilt, cursing myself for an impulse that I should have known would land me in the shit, I fumble out from under the blanket and make for the corner of the paddock where the goats have huddled in a final stand. My bladder is full and I piss with an exuberance that is far removed from how I feel, but the goats seem to relate to it and go back to their grazing as though I had proven to be of their primordial kin. A pom, whose face I have seen but whose name I do not know, is crapping nearby, his lard-white buttocks splayed, his hands bearing down on his knees and his face contorted like a woman in labour as he urges out the finger-thin turd of the semi-starved. I turn away, feeling sicker than I was, as he begins to wipe his arse with a snatch of the grass and see Douglas sitting up in his blanket in the place which we had decided would be ours, and am sure that he has seen me too, because he at once begins to babble and gesture with a vivaciousness that is as pathetic as it is alienating, and sometimes he pushes at the still blanketed form beside him and laughs, his head thrown back and his mouth as gaping as a hole.

'Like a whore,' I think and go back to where Danny is now sitting on the edge of the blanket and staring at the grass between his toes, and think to greet him, but then decide that I won't, will wait instead to see if he will do so first, but he gets up and brushes past me and, like me, goes to piss, and I steel myself for the outburst and final bust-up that must surely come when he returns. But then the Ites are fanning our clothes out all over the grass and shouting that we have an hour to get dressed before they herd us back to camp, and there is a milling and bickering that brings out the beast in us as we try to identify what is ours, and, once, two poms even come to blows, but, all the time I am searching, finding, shrugging on, I am thinking, 'Christ! What do I do now? Go back to Douglas with no card to play? Walk on my knees?' and again I am trying to find a hatred for Danny as I watch him pawing over the clothes, the very twist and stoop of his still naked back telling me I am dung.

Clothes found, I start to walk over to where we are forming up according to the huts to which we belong, and Danny is closing up on me from behind, is walking alongside me, is touching my arm, is saying in a tone that leaves no distance between us, 'See you later, mate?' and I nod, not daring to say anything because whatever I say will be saying too much, but I do lightly punch his arm and he goes into boxer-stance, then swerves away to join the poms.

The Ites count us, panic, count us again, then start us walking back to the camp, but I make no attempt to latch onto Douglas and, in fact, could not do that even if I would because *he* has latched onto whoever it is that shared his blanket if the over-loud dialogue is to be believed. Covertly I study the guy, wondering why I don't know him if he is from our hut, then *do* recognize him as one of the stagehands with quarters in the theatre who – because he was the *only* one from the theatre to be infested – was allowed to tag onto whatever group he pleased. A sallow youth with long hair but no beard, pointy elfin ears and a narrow-eyed narrow face redeemed only by a lush, almost womanly-red mouth, he is not my cup of tea and I can't imagine him really being Douglas' either, but, charade or not, preference or not, I am not caring two fucks any more about *anything* Douglas does.

Back in the hut, we don't speak to each other, don't even *look* at each other, and I grab my sliver of soap and tatty towel and hurry down to the ablution block to bath under a tap before every other lousy bastard gets the same idea, which adjective, I notice with relief after washing my crotch clear of whatever the white powder was, no longer applies. Then Douglas, pointedly waiting till I return, goes to bath and, at chow call, we, for the first time ever, each fetch our own swill and eat it each in our own bunk, after which I hang up my still – pointedly – unwashed dixie and turn over to get some much-needed *proper* kip.

But Douglas is having none of it. Balancing on the edge of the interloper's bunk – he, for once, not being there – he addresses my back, his voice unsteady but not giving in. 'Why did you make such a fool of me last night? What did I do to you that you should hurt me like you did?'

The namby-pamby second question at once ignites me like a match a flare. 'What do you mean – *hurt* you? You seemed to be having a good enough time with what you picked up! And, anyway, I *told* you what it was all about.'

'You lied, Tom. Lied like you did about the shorts. And about you not seeing who hugged you after the show. And about your not waking me to hear that bird sing. All this time, Tom, you have been lying and lying while you have been running after that what's-his-name who, I am now sure, was the one you had in mind when you wanted us to open up our laundry business and you fed me that fancy talk about infrastructure when all you wanted was to have *him* with you all the time.'

'*That* is where you made your big mistake! If you had let him in instead of reacting like a jealous wife, maybe you and I wouldn't be breaking up the way we are now.'

'So you're saying it – openly – at last? That we're breaking up? That that is what you want?'

'Well, what does it look like to you? That we are on our second honeymoon?'

'Stop *talking* like that! This is not the time for stupid jokes!'

'Who says I am joking? I am giving it to you *straight*.'

For a moment he is silent and even my back knows that I have cut him down, that he is slithering about as in a flood of tears still struggling to be shed. But he tries again, game to the end – or just unable to accept that the show is over and the world on the stage is back to being painted cardboard and prettied-up wood? 'How can you possibly so soon forget? Does it mean nothing to you that I cleaned you up each time you dirtied yourself in that horrible boat, that I worked it so that we got double rations at the infirmary down south, that I was there with the aspirins when that stupid dentist would have let you bleed to death, and again, only the other day, when that guard would have beaten you to a pulp if I hadn't chased him away? What sort of a man *are* you that you now can turn your back on me as if I'm trash?'

Now I am seeing red, can hardly wait for him to

take a breath. 'What is it, then, that you want? *Payment* for favours done?'

'You *know* I'm not wanting that. All I'm asking is that you have the decency to stick with someone who has stuck with you and not go running off with every new pair of fancy pants.'

'Jesus Christ!' and now I whip around, almost incoherent with rage. 'Who the fuck are you to talk to me as though I'm some kind of a rough stud? Don't forget it's not *me* that hitched up with *you*, but the other way around. I never *wanted* you for a mate, did my best to give you the slip, but you kept on sucking up to me like a goddam tick till I gave up and let you have your way. And, talking about payment for favours, let me remind you that I beat up that poor mad wanker for wanting to take away your beads and, while you're throwing a favour here and a favour there in my face, *I* have been doing *you* a favour *all the time* by letting you mother me like a little girl getting her kicks out of her doll!'

'Why, you filthy beast!' he almost shrieks and the hut is all ears. 'I have got a good mind to – to –'

'To what, you bloody old cow?' I howl. 'You couldn't hurt pussy, let alone anything with balls! Now get the fuck away from me before I kick you in the teeth!'

His face disappears at that and I strain to hear if there will be any sounds of incontinent grief since such a sissyness will entrench me in my anger and contempt, but the silence below is so accusingly stoical and profound that I begin to feel several kinds of a heel, though not for long, my relief at the severance of the umbilical cord too overwhelming to be that easily subdued.

The next two days I spend with Danny, partly because that is where I want to be and partly because living with Douglas is like a killer cohabiting with the victim of his crime. I do not tell Danny anything about what is going on because I am still not sure what the final outcome will be, but, at chow time of the third day, when I go to fetch my dixie from our hut, Douglas' bunk is stripped and what I am sure is the exact half of our remaining stock of Red Cross food and cigarettes is laid out on mine. Only then, staring at the abandoned bunk, do I fleetingly but sincerely grieve, and only then do I tell Danny all, and he looks at me as though assessing me for any lingering regrets, then nods and swats at a particularly pestiferous fly.

The next day, more curious than concerned, I visit Tony and he looks at me as I walk in and at once says, 'Yes, he's here and if you're worried – which I doubt – then don't be, because we look after our own.'

Then I bribe the hut boss with the cigarettes that Douglas left and he fixes it so that Danny can move in, and, in a final act of irony, the interloper moves downstairs so that Danny can have his bunk and almost smiles as he says that maybe he always wanted the bottom bunk anyway.

━━━━►●◄━━━━

As if by mutual agreement, Douglas and I keep out of one another's way as much as that is possible in a camp as crowded as ours, but I still often see him, either from afar or relatively near, and usually he is with the sallow youth who seems animated and dependent enough to make him a better companion for Douglas than I ever

could have been. As for Danny and me, the new and
constant closeness does not pose any problems or throw
up any disillusionments because we acknowledge that
we are both solitary birds and respect each other's occasional urge to stand on one leg and alone. Also, we share
the barely controlled sloppiness common to most 'bach-
elors' which, to me, is a relief after Douglas' fussiness,
as it is a relief to be rid of the incessant chatter to which
his new companion appears to be equally prone. There
are, of course, the bouts of snappishness that empty
stomachs breed, but Danny's innate sense of fun always
restores the equilibrium and is bringing out in me a capacity for laughter that I never knew was mine. Whether
the never discussed night in the 'decontamination' paddock has anything to do with it, I shall never know, but
it is so that we are increasingly also easier with each
other in the *physical* sense, often draping an arm about
a neck or jabbing an elbow into a side, and sometimes
we even wrestle a little as kids do, getting to know each
other's texture and smell, but that does not happen too
often, the boniness of us warningly in the way.

Then, perplexingly, there is a shifting in the pattern
of our lives, an almost crackling in the air as though a
log jam is yielding to a flowing's urge.

There is another unexpected distribution of parcels
though no Red Cross trucks are seen to be entering or
leaving the camp – something, this, which our greedy
vigilance would never have missed – and, even more in-
explicably, there is suddenly meat in the swill and, on
odd days, a truly generous chunk each of the tangy Ite
cheese. Food aside, the Ites themselves are getting

weird, the guards nodding and grinning and trading their wretched English across the fences with none of the mercenary intentions to which we are used; and we are still asking each other, 'What the fuck is *going on*?' when, on a night, what seems to be all the church bells in the world are clanging like crazy, and sounding louder and louder, till we are thinking the churches are marching up over the hills to squat around the camp, and all the Madonnas will be waving from the windows and smiling their sad not-saying-anything smiles.

And then the bugle is blaring for us to assemble at the gates, and the commandant is climbing up onto one of the observation towers, loud-hailer in hand, but no interpreter, and a searchlight from the barracks is swivelling across to spotlight him, and he stands there, looking a little lost and not at all like the boss man we thought we knew. We hush and he speaks, his English – *English*? – 'Sly old bastard,' Danny whispers in my ear – broken and halting but wholly intelligible, and we hear that the war is over, for the Ites at any rate, and the gates will be left open as of now, but we are advised to stay close to the camp because there are marauding bands about and our people can at any time arrive to organize our going home. Meanwhile, he adds, our link man will arrange for the distribution of the last of the parcels which he has been holding in the store that we might celebrate this night in style – 'Fucking old liar,' Danny again whispers, but there is more of affection than venom in the words – and there is vino for the taking at the barracks, but our own men must staff the canteen so that the wine can be served to us in a manner befitting gentlemen and – he pauses – winners in war. Then he salutes, quickly, his calm coming apart at the seams, and the light switches off and he might never have been.

For a moment, we stand, buttocks to crotch, irresolute and stunned as at a tidings of death, not joy. Then a roar erupts, and I hear myself yelling, and Danny is kissing me on the lips, and I am kissing him back and knowing no discomfort at that, it seeming the inevitable and only way to say what heart and tongue can no longer hold.

Not all of us behave like 'gentlemen and winners in war'. Some take bunks and bedding from the huts and set them alight and dance around the flames till exhaustion and drunkenness drag them down. Others wander aimlessly through the flickering dark, grinning with the vacuous delight of the insane and uttering meaningless cries, and some few have to be cast off from their slobbering latching onto every passing neck, huge eyes begging proof that they do not dream. The Ite guards join in, stripping off their badges of unit and rank, handing them out as souvenirs, sometimes brandishing flagons of wine in excess of the canteen's, passing these around, themselves drinking till they reel in a bizarre delirium of love for the once loathed. Churned up by the milling feet, dust clouds the camp in a pale, peppery mist through which we blunder or prowl, mutter or howl, appear, disappear, like guilt-ridden ghosts, and sometimes fight, settling old scores in a bloodying with fists that turns the festivities into nightmare and victory into defeat.

Some hours before dawn, the camp at last stills, many sleeping where they dropped, and Danny and I, tipsy as any and meeting again after having been parted by the crowd, help each other up onto my bunk where we lie together, grinning into each other's faces like lobotomized fools. Then the grins fade as we succumb to what we have all the time suppressed – the knowledge that our freedom is synonymous with our separation, that, within days, maybe even in the morning, we will be parted to be flown, or shipped, back to where we belong, the oceans endlessly between. 'So the bitter Eden ends,' I think. 'So *fucking* soon,' and I feel my mouth twist and he touches it with as grieving a hand. Then we turn into each other, breath to breath, and sleep, entwined.

Sun high, we wake, go out, come quickly back in. The Jerries have moved in from the north, are ringing the camp, are lining up the commandant and the guards, and the first shots ring out even as we huddle down onto the interloper's bunk, he nowhere to be found. 'Christ,' says Danny and we stare at each other as though it's the first time. Then he remembers something, and feels in the two baggy pockets of the old tunic he is wearing, and takes out two Ite service pistols and hands me one.

'A souvenir,' he says and actually grins.

'Where did you get these?' Astonished, I gape as though he had put a snake in my hand.

'When we got split up last night, I went over to the barracks to see if you were there, and these two Ite brass were getting out of their gear and into civvies, but *fast*, meaning to make for the hills and home. So they toss me these two guns because they don't want to maybe be caught with them and be found out for what they were.'

'So why give *me* one? You wanting us to take on the Jerry army on our own?'

'No, mate, I was going to give you one, anyway. To take home, like I said, for a souvenir. But now I'm mostly giving it because it will be easier for me to get one past the Jerries than two. Which goes for you as well.'

'*No way* will we get them through! Not even with one.'

'I think we can. There's a lot of blokes that's got to go through those gates and I can see the Krauts maybe searching our balls, but I can't see them going through our *kit*. Not with our guys already on their tail. So we stuff them deep and have a go.'

I consider that while he watches me, then he says with an earnestness that compels, stirs the primal roots of my hairs, 'Look, Tom, these are not the desert blokes that were not so bad. These are the spit-and-polish boys from home base and the story goes that they are *prime* turds. So we don't know how many kinds of hell may be waiting for us out there and we may be glad someday that we stashed a bullet that can end it for us like you end it for a dog that's been run over in the road.'

'Proper little ray of sunshine, *you* are!' I try to mock, but I am still hearing those shots outside and my flesh crawls.

'Don't, mate,' he warns and his voice is quiet, yet it

tears through me like a yell. 'I don't know how much *real* action you've seen and I don't *want* to know. But don't forget I was with the tanks and we didn't sit around polishing our guns. I've seen dead men and I have seen men dying with their guts hanging out and begging for a bullet in the brain. So try and get your gun through and don't waste the bullet it's loaded with now because there are no more where it came from, and you never know.'

He sits quietly, then, his eyes neutral and calm, waiting for me to decide, and at last I get up and stash the gun at the bottom of the hulk's bag.

'Tell me,' I say when he has also hidden his and we are back on the bottom bunk, 'what would you do if I *did* put a bullet in my brain?' and I am regretting the question even as I ask it because it is a cheap shot aimed at starting a sloppy exchange, but he considers it carefully and with that dispassion that I have come to realize is the other side of the coin.

'I would follow you,' he says, his voice matter-of-fact as though he is saying he will join me on a walk, which is perhaps exactly what he *does* mean, he adding, 'Death is no big deal when it's a bullet in the brain. Now you're here, now you are flesh and blood. Boom-bang and you're on the other side, and, though I'm no choirboy, I think there *is* an other side because too many blokes were going out as though they were seeing things.'

'But what about your mum? Your wife? Would you not be thinking about them?'

'Sure, I'd be thinking about them, but in my own way, and if there wasn't that own way, I wouldn't be sitting alongside of *you* now. Take my missus. Sure, I love her and if we had had a kid, I might not be giving you the answer I'm giving you now. I don't know. But I *do* know that she's got a better graft than me and she would get herself another man if I died, like I would get myself another wife if *she* died. But a mate, who's been through a war or the camps with you, is the *only* one of his kind, like a mum is the only one of *her* kind. But *me* mum' – is the 'me' instead of 'my' a slip of the tongue or a surfacing of a deeper he? – 'is old and could be gone before I ever get out of here, but meantime she has her pension and her house and she is the one who would *best* understand. My mum has been a great mum and my missus has been a great missus, so they'll be OK when they get on that other side, but my poor mate who's shot himself, *he* will be wandering about on his own, all shaken up and reaching out for his other half that's still back here. Which other half is *me*.'

I stare at him, stunned by the wild, relentless splendour of his world, longing to be of it, yet cravenly afraid.

As relentlessly as his world, he probes, 'You would do the same for me?'

Automaton, though still fiercely *wanting*, I nod and he seizes my hand.

'Swear?' he insists, and again I nod, feeling *his* wanting flood into me through his hand, and his face opens and I walk into his world.

Then the Krauts, as distinct from the Jerries, are screaming, 'Raus! Raus!' and by nightfall we are down at the little station beyond the hill and are being crammed into the waiting cattle-trucks like sausage meat into its skin, and, sometime in the far night, Danny beside me and the guns still undetected in our gear, I feel the trucks shudder and sway as they labour over the mountains into Krautland, the ice and snow on the towering peaks singing like devils as they thread through our bones.

———————

We have lost all sense of space and time, the significance of what we pass, only peripherally observe. Pines, stark as pikes, approach, recede, as though it is *they* that move, tell us that there is a perspective to the white paper of the snow, but we, too, are paper, *stay* paper, two-dimensionally and blessedly unaware. Each day we slosh through the snow that is not snow, each night lie down in it, the flakes covering us like the bugs in that land, now two years dead, where I cannot remember it ever having rained, though, of course, it did, the unchanging sun shining in my mind alone.

How slowly, prissily, we move, putting each foot down as though its bones are broken or a priceless glass, but the guards don't seem to mind, seem to understand that we are barely this side of sense, that no amount of shouting, or belabouring with rifle-butts, will quicken flesh already busied with its death. The two loaves of bread, dozen boiled potatoes and a Red Cross food parcel each with which we started out have long since been desperately, sparingly, eaten and returned to the earth in the shape of our minute, difficult turds, and all that is left to us are the occasional, seemingly abandoned turnip fields that the guards permit us to rifle, phlegmatically watching as we claw out the turning-woody turnips and gnaw at them with teeth that, each day, seem less rooted in our gums.

We ask the guards how much further and they shrug. We ask them what *is* the purpose of the march and, mostly, they again shrug, but some say we *are* going to a better camp down south, but don't look at us while they are saying this, a tightness to their mouths that disturbs. We pass through a city which we are dimly aware has fallen in upon itself like a pack of cards, only a cathedral's steeple still standing as though it witnessed to the indestructibility of truth – or is it myth? – and people are scuttling in and out of the ruins and going about their business with the imperviousness of ants, and we ask the guards what city is this, but now they do not shrug *or* answer, just look at us with a loathing that rears its head with the swiftness and deadliness of a snake.

Each night, bodies thick as slugs with all the clothing we still possess, Danny and I bed down together, grappling each other for warmth with the awkwardness of mating snails, and sometimes we fumble back through the two years since we rocked down the last gradient into a countryside of lawns that were virgin grass, and storybook houses for pixies and elves, and we rank and sodden from lying, interlaced as packaged fish, in the shit and piss that anxious anuses and bladders were no longer able to restrain. It is then that we realize that the past can be as truly past as it is truly present, so much of it already fading from the immediate memory like a writing in water or sand, but that which remains as vividly terrible or pleasant as though yesterday and today were forever one, and Danny tells me that his mum says that, now that she is growing old, she is remembering yesterday more wholly and frighteningly than today.

There is no consistency or predictability, though, in what we recall. I will mention something that I think, laughingly – or as close to a laugh as I can still get – is trivial and he will think it meaningful, or he will mention something that he thinks is meaningful and I will think it's trivial, and so it goes. All, though, from a tapestry of the past that, whether agonizing or satisfying, is preferable to the intolerable present, not to speak of a future which seems to hold in it more of death than life, and there is a time in which I whisper – hardly daring to speak even that softly of it – that maybe we should use the bullets to end it now. But Danny does not answer and we go on plucking bits and pieces from nostalgia's shrivelling flesh, trying to find in them a sequentiality less final than the now forebodes – trying, impossibly, to forget.

So we are back in the cattle-trucks, lolloping to the camp on a remote eastern border that we left Christ knows how many aeons ago now, but half-way we stop, the night stretched thin, are shunted off onto a side-track, the sounds of a city widely around, but the truck itself, after the clash of couplings, screeching of wheels, seeming to hold in a sweet power of silence that overrides all outer noise. Heaving up out of the sleeping crush of bodies on the floor, Danny and I stay where we stand, knowing that if we don't we will never be able to lie down again, and peer through the truck's air vents at leaves scuttling across streetlights and know from that that our planes are here still but a rumouring of the wind. Further off is an intense wash of blue-white light under a roof's iron overhang, and there is a ceaseless clangour as of a thousand tinsmiths banging on their anvils, and a harsh Kraut voice, magnified to that of a god or demon, is exhorting the workers to greater efforts in the cause of the Reich that will last a thousand years.

'Shit!' I whisper to Danny. 'A thousand years in a cattle-truck!' and laugh, but there is hysteria in the laugh, but he whispers back that there is still the bullet for the brain and there is no hysteria in *him*. Then, suddenly, a sheet-white face is looking up from a clot of darkness that could be a hat or scarf, and a hand is reaching up, proffering, urging that we take what it holds, and I do and face and hand are gone, soundlessly as they came. Carefully, I feel, smell, touch my tongue to what the hand gave and my starving stomach – the commandant never having had the chance to distribute the promised parcels before they shot him dead – knows it for what it is. 'Eat!' it yells and I whisper-shout to Danny, *'Bacon!'* and we take turns lingeringly nibbling at the rich, raw fat and lean meat, then halve the six by two inches of rind and chew on it till no taste is left, then wolf it down whole.

The eastern border turns out to be, as Danny pungently puts it, the unwiped arsehole of the world. Flat, dispiriting plains stretch to as dispiriting skylines, the monotony broken, although hardly inspiringly so, by occasional plantations of regimented pines, or frowsty huddles of indigenous woods so small that one leaves as one enters, and, worst of all, stacks of sudden factories from which billow endless streamers of oily and contaminating smoke. 'They boil the corpses there,' quips one wag, humour not yet quite dead, and we laugh, but with a shudder down the spine.

The camp, though, is not all that bad, is in fact better than the Ites', though some of the elements are the same. Long barracks-like buildings of sooty but decently-laid brick house many hundreds of men, but there is an ablution and laundering room in the centre of each and the several outside toilets, though still open-pit with multiple seats, are roofed and durable structures that invite the illusion that one is crapping in a slightly less barbarous style. Bunks are again three-tiered, but somewhat wider with wider aisles between, and Danny and I push, then shove, until he gets the bottom and I the middle bunk in the same tier.

Outside, cobbled paths crisscross between the blocks with the mathematical exactness that the Krauts so love, and we are each issued, amazingly, with a pair of wooden clogs, which we at once put on so as to prolong the life of our already worse for wear, once forever army boots, then clack around on the cobbles uneasily and gigglingly as little kids trying out their roller skates for the first time. Beyond one of the two longer fences, with their mandatory barbs and searchlights on heron-like towers, is a plantation of pines that, should the wind be right, aromatically brood on their precisely-spaced shadows and out of which a woodcutter, or

whatever, will sometimes suddenly emerge, look startled and flee.

The food is partly better, partly horrendously worse
than the Ites', but there is more of it and there are two
feeding periods a day. In the morning, we get a hunk
each of coarse black bread and a half a dixie of saccha-
rin-sweetened coffee which those in the know say is
brewed from acorns – or is it chestnuts? – but, whichever, has certainly never known a coffee-bean; and, at
any time after noon, we get a dixie of turnip swill –
which is as execrable as it sounds and goes to ground
under a yellow scum if you let it stand too long – plus
a handful of potatoes boiled in their skins, a medallion
of 'cheese' which smells like rotting fish or feet, a pat of
'butter' which again the know-alls say is made from
coal and evaporates as summarily as water should you
melt it for a fry, and a tablespoon of jam that really *is*
made from sugar beet and is the closest to being OK.
But why not all this together with the *bread*?

The mysterious 'cheese', however, is what intrigues
us the most and Danny and I who, like many others,
have managed to bring our blower-stove with us, take it,
a dixie, a lick of margarine from the Red Cross parcels –
which seem to be more regular here – and a round of
the 'cheese' which we then try to 'toast' in the margarine, and end up with a gummy mess that surely can only
be molten animal horn? Worst of all, it takes forever to
get the dixie clean again and it is the one 'food' that,
eventually, *no one* – not even the ex-magistrate, which
says it all – any longer wants to have, and Danny's bunk
is shaking with his whooping it up when I suggest that,

in the toilet's noisome depths, there must by this time surely be a *mountain* of discarded 'cheese' that, horror-movie-wise, is slyly mutating into the monster that yet, like the rats in Iteland, will have us by our balls.

Children of colonizers, we, too, are colonizers to the manner born, bringing with us not only our blower-stoves, but all the rest of the infrastructure which we need to found a new and, hopefully, less bitter Eden in which we can live, or, unbiblically, die. So, almost from touchdown, the old systems are again being put in place: the gambling kings, bleary-eyed and bitter-lipped, slapping down their cards till late, the mini-traders, ebullient and eloquent, touting their wares, the laundry-men licking arses for work, Tony negotiating with the Krauts for a theatre and getting it, and Camel chancing his arm with an 'exhibition' of drawings of nude groins – 'Pay your cigarette before you look,' says the notice tacked to his bunk – but no one heeds, there being enough naked cocks around for free.

One thing that *cannot* be revived, however, is the camp band, our last sighting of the instruments being when – shortly before our leaving for the cattle-trucks the other side of the hill – they were being loaded onto a Kraut truck and destined for anywhere save here. But a revival that gladdens me most is when Danny starts slowly but steadily running again, the relatively generous quantities of solid if often unpalatable food putting a little flesh back on his bones.

Then there is also the wholly new activity of classes, which the several civvy street teachers in our midst offer to give for a variety of reasons ranging from nostalgia to keeping their hand in to simply slaughtering time. I opt for the German language classes, partly because it might be useful, although in what *way* – philosophical discussions with the Kommandant? – I am not at all sure, and partly because German sounds like Afrikaans and should be the easy way to go, and somehow I stick to it even when I find out that *a fork* is female and *a spoon* is male. 'For Chrissakes,' I say to Danny, 'surely that should be the other way around?' Danny, however, astonishes me by choosing botany and goes around mumbling Latin names for shrubs and flowers he has never seen – or perhaps has but didn't know – and when I ask him, 'Why *botany?*' stressing the word as though it is a slug on my tongue, he explains, silencing me, that there is a field behind their house that's full of flowers in spring and learning about 'flowers and stuff' will remind him of home.

On a more practical level, a Spam-and-potato potency sparking in me as in Danny, I decide to go back into the laundry business and wheedle Danny into siding with me in this, although I will not allow myself to be persuaded to run. He makes it clear, though, that he is only going along with the idea because, even if he said 'No,' he would still be sharing in the material benefits accruing from my sweat and that would make him feel like – as he puts it – a kept man. So I find myself working with the human equivalent of a racehorse hitched to a plough – or, to put it less poetically, an incurably embarrassed grumbler who moans all the time that washing is for women, not men, and, in the end, I give up on him and solve the problem of the kept man by telling him that he can be the manager – hanging up the washing for drying, taking it down again, folding it, delivering it, extorting payment like extracting teeth, negotiating new business, and any number of other duties that will be a sop to his pride and still have us together in our increasing clinging to each other like two castaways in a tricky sea.

'Well, if only one of us is to be the woman in this deal, then it looks like it's got to be me,' I pretend to, in my turn, complain, and his eyes flick down, and as slyly up, as he hits back, 'Pity it's the wrong waterworks or we could have us a ball.'

For a moment, I don't get it, then do and an original me rears, outraged, then as quickly is felled and I am laughing without strain.

'So!' I taunt, a triumphalism in me that I do not quite understand, cannot control. 'How now your story about the right hole?'

'Blokes and bints don't feel the same,' he grunts. 'A bloke can take what's on the plate and nothing's changed,' and again he glances down as though at balls not seen, then turns, sharply, away. 'What *is* this?' the far-off me again exclaims, not so much because of what it has heard, but because of a sudden gush of warmth where no warmth should be.

Five minutes later, he is back, the flaming shape I had sensed in him quite gone. Or has it never been there, my mind alone the flaming giveaway? 'I found the old staff that gave me his bunk,' he says, his voice glad. 'Same old sod he always was. Says to come over sometime so's he can grab your hand.'

That pleases me as much as it pleases Danny because the once *bête noire* had become the almost-friend that he would *allow* anyone to become, but we never saw him again after the Krauts took over and feared him dead as the poor Ite guards the Krauts left lying where they fell. That, I am thinking, completes a circle, chinks a missing link in place, and I am still feeling good about it when, washing on alone and Danny gone to fetch the chow, I have this feeling that I am being watched – not incuriously so, but with the intensity of a sorrowing or a rage – and I turn, quickly, to the grimy window close beside me and Douglas is walking away in the direction of the theatre with the stiffness of back and quickness of step of one who nearly waited too long.

⸺⸻⸺

Autumn eases into winter and the first snow, then come the heavier and boringly endless falls that burden the branches of the pines till, sometimes in the crystal nights, they snap with the loudness of shots and their loads come whooshing down in a feathery roar. The cobbled paths turn smooth and slippery as glass and there are serious tumbles as we grapple with the clogs, and Danny soon learns that if he leaves the washing out to dry after the sun has reached a certain low, he will have to wrestle it into the barracks and stack it like boards to the accompaniment of furious cries. He also learns that when the temperature shafts us with a particular spite, the only solution is to clamber up into my bunk without a by-my-leave, shove me aside and wrap me round as though he would be my second skin, but I am not complaining, am in my secret self even now knowing that I will be missing this when summer comes.

Winter also brings letters – shoals of them – as though all of autumn's dammed-up leaves have suddenly broken free. Some of them are so old, tell of emotions, deeds, events, so long past, that they are more histories written by dead hands than the voices of the living reaching out to the still alive. But they are still read, smelt, carefully folded, as carefully again unfolded to be again read, then at last laid aside with the reverence due to icons, or the dead.

Danny gets nine letters – five from his mother, four from his wife. They are his first letters since the Krauts hauled him, virtually unhurt, from his mangled tank. He stares at them, holding them, fanned, in both his hands, his eyes bemused with disbelief – then he very quietly gets up and goes away to some far corner of the camp, his letters tightly clasped as though they might take wing, and stays away for so long that I grow restless with a loneliness that is the other face of dread.

Then he is back, incandescent with the need to share, and begins to read me passages from his letters, and goes on and on, but I am staring at my empty hands, empty because – because of what? – my never having given enough of myself to anyone for them to want to give me anything back? I shy away from the question and he reads on, and I'm thinking I will get up and walk out of here, but then understanding comes to him and he puts his letters away and does me a dozen small favours to *show* me that he understands, but I hold out for nearly too long, guiltily but unyieldingly aware that what I am *now* feeling is the sullen jealousy of the brat I have never outgrown.

Some days later, Tony sends me a message that he would like to see me – the first such message to come from him since we arrived – and, curious, I lose no time in getting down to the theatre to which I have but infrequently been, and then only when there is a show, I not wanting to risk running into Douglas again. It is about the size of the one the Ites gave us, only longer and narrower, being half of a barracks with the backing ablution and laundry room serving as a storeroom for costumes, sets and general theatre bric-à-brac. The stage – contrived with the usual cunning from packing cases supplied by the Krauts and with a worn but authentic stage curtain also supplied by the Krauts who seem to be as weirdly culture-conscious as the Ites – is sited in front of the storeroom, which then also doubles as a dressing-room for the more brash than bashful performers and provides them with an easy entrance to the stage. In the other half of the barracks, Tony has ensconced himself in a private space behind a stack of sheets of cardboard that were supposed to have been converted into sets, while the considerable rest of the room has been turned into a dormitory of individual beds for stagehands, set designers, make-up artistes and an assortment of hangers-on who snuff the corruption-tainted air with the challenging brazenness of their kind.

Arrived, I find Tony sitting reading on a chair he has taken from those stacked against the 'auditorium' walls, and he at once gets up, closing his book with the brisk snap that is his way and seizing my hand with an almost-unctuousness that is *not* his way. Then he leads me over the stage, arousing in me – purposely? – surprisingly sharp memories of the one and only show in which I have ever been, and on into his 'space' which contains no more than a bed that is no more than a cot, a crude bar stool and as crude a something like a what-not that he has stuffed with books, papers, clothes.

'Sit down,' he says, hooking the stool forward with his foot, and I do and he goes out and comes back with two mugs of tea with sugar *and* milk, and hands me one before he sits down on the bed.

'How do you like my pad?'

'No frills,' I say and cannot keep the surprise from my voice.

'Typical of you straights!' he snorts, then adds, 'That is if you *are* still straight,' and chuckles contentedly when I frown. 'Always expecting fruits to be lolling on silk doodahs and indulging in orgies they wouldn't mind trying out themselves.' Then he looks at me, measuredly, as though seeing me for the first time, and, in his turn, frowns. 'Happy,' he says, addressing himself rather than me, 'but going to seed,' and I know that he is referring to my hair and beard which, although reasonably under control, are not as neatly trimmed as in that other time and place, the barbering business being the one activity that has only minimally survived as a result of the Krauts' refusing to help out with equipment as did the Ites and the few barbers who managed to smuggle out their scissors having to use only these to lop off what they can.

'But I can soon fix that. For Danny too, if he

wants,' and he looks at me expectantly, but I don't answer him, knowing that I wouldn't get Danny here
even if I *dragged* him by his too long hair, and try to
conceal my uneasiness as I sip my tea and listen to the
chatter of voices and bustle of bodies the other side of
the cardboard wall.

But the owlish eyes behind the glittering pince-nez
miss nothing, as I should have known. 'He's not here,'
he says, simply, almost sympathetically. 'I sent him out
on an errand, knowing how you would feel.'

I should feel gratitude, but don't, only say, my
voice harsh with the shyness of being exposed, 'OK,
Tony. Cut the offers and the tea. What is it that you
want to wheedle out of me?'

Again he chuckles, this time appreciatively, but does
not at once answer, looking past me as though I am not
there, his face its usual glum façade. 'I'm going to try
something new,' he at last explains. 'So far, the shows
we have put on – like the one you were in back there –
were either serious plays with all-male casts or they
were farces where the guys playing the parts of the
women were clearly still guys doing it for the audience
to laugh at and have fun. Now I want to put on a serious play with men playing the parts of women as
though they *were* women and not men.'

He looks at me, clearly expecting some profundity,
but the presentation is still too sudden, too raw, and
the best I can manage is, 'Such as?'

'Old Bill Shakespeare's Macbeth,' and now I do
react, but with consternation and no small measure of
distaste, and he goes on, 'I know exactly what you are

going to say – that Shakespeare is dead meat, that the audience will boo the cast off the stage and come wanting to cut off my balls. But I am going to do it like it's never been done before – shove the bloodshed and the witches and the ghost out front like a whore her cunt, and even slice out some of the lines if there is no other way. In short, my friend, I am going to turn Macbeth into the highfalutin thriller that it really is and have those slobs out there panting for the visuals, but also slotting into the lines because they will want to know what is going on.'

I am listening, but with gathering admiration now, beginning to nod, beginning to see what he sees. Then I am thinking of the characters in the play, trying to remember the little that I learnt of it at school. 'The head heavy that wanted to chicken out? The butch missus that didn't give a fuck? Christ, Tony, these were *psychos*! You got guys that can handle *them*?'

He is pleased, slaps my knee. 'We already have Macbeth – long, sly shit that *always* looks that way and only has to narrow his eyes and he's *right*. He churns out his lines like they're a mantra, but, as I said, we'll pile on the visuals till nobody cares a fuck *what* he says.'

'And the wife?'

'You,' he says and looks at me with such a matter-of-factness that, for a moment, I do not grasp what he has said. Then I do and stand up, saying something like, 'Thanks for the tea,' and make to leave, but he holds me back, seats me again on the stool. 'Wait, man, wait! Don't be in such a hurry! At least *think* about it before you say "No!".'

'What is there to think *about*? Do *you* think I'm one of your pervs that's going to prance around on that stage in a fucking *dress*?'

Anger, I all too miserably know, is making me say things that I should not, that I will regret, but he does not take offence. 'Lady M does not *prance*, Tom. She is a *queen*. What is more, she will be wearing a queen's robe that we will see to it covers everything except your face and hands, and even your hands we will be shoving into gloves if they look too much like a man's, which I am sure they do, and as for your face, we will do that over till, when you look in a mirror, you will feel *inside* that you are a *queen* rather than a woman, and every-body out there will be seeing you in that same way and not one, I can guarantee you, will be wanting to take you to bed after the show!'

'So if it's that easy, why don't you try your tricks on some other goon? Why pick on me?'

Quietly, his eyes insist that I listen, heed. 'Do you re-member your death scene in that other play and how I battled to make you whisper so that the whole audience could hear, and how, on opening night, you suddenly got it right and never looked back till the end of the run?' I do not even bother to nod, and he goes on, 'Well, one of *the* crucial scenes in Macbeth is when wifey walks in her sleep and speaks to the blood on her hands, and I want her to *whisper* those words as you did then, as only you can do now, and *that* is why I am *begging* you to not let me down, to say yes, you will do that for me this one more time!'

'Great speech,' I sneer, but already I am feeling the

net of my vanity closing around me and I not trying
hard enough to get out from under it, and already I am
seeing myself playing the part of the Queen and hearing
myself imposing only the one condition: that it be left
to me to 'go public' – by which I mean to tell Danny –
in my own time and my own way.

'Sure,' he says and shakes my hand, trying not to
look as victorious as he feels. He also, on my way out,
hands me two Red Cross parcels which a skivvy brings,
explaining, deadpan, 'To fatten you up a bit. Wifey was
no pale Ophelia. Probably packed a wallop like a
man's,' and he looks at me and I look at him, but still do
not know which it is – the truth or a bribe? – but also
do not really care, only ask him for something to put
them in for carrying through a camp that's all eyes.

Danny's not there when I get back, as I half-expected
would be the case, he not one for lolling around in his
bunk, even when it is as cold as it is now and most do.
So I shove the parcels in under his bunk and sit down
on it and ask myself how and when to tell Danny what,
sooner or later, I must, and at once know that I have
not even *begun* to think this thing through, that the
'how' – and 'how *much*' – may still demand of me an
answering, but the '*when*' is *right now*. How can I possibly delay telling him the nature of my business with
Tony when we are so interlocked, the one with the
other, that we even say, 'I'm going for a shit' when we
are going for a shit? Not only that, but Tony has –
knowingly or unknowingly? – trapped me with the parcels under the bunk. How can I remain silent about
*them*? Panic mounting, I turn to the 'how' and 'how

much' and am again trapped. I could tell him about
the play without telling him what *role* I am going to
play, but how long before it all leaks out in a camp that
is as much all ears as it is all eyes and I then stand ac-
cused of a duplicity that will lose me Danny's trust as
though it had never been?

I am still no nearer a solution, when he walks in,
raised eyebrow asking 'Well?', and I hear myself saying,
instinctively and without fuss, 'Tony has offered me a
part in his new play.'

'So? Would he be wanting you for anything *else*?'
There is a snideness to the question that I do not miss,
but I let it pass.

'First payment,' I add, scrabbling the parcels out
from under his bunk, awkwardly offering them as to an
unpredictable god.

He nudges them with his foot. 'Looks good. So
you're saying you said "Yes"?'

'Would you mind?'

'Nah, not *much*. You're my mate and you know I
don't like sharing you with those theatre creeps, but
you did fine in that other play and I can see it's what
you like to do, like I like to run. So, OK. Let the cam-
eras roll.'

Now he is almost jocular and I make for what I
think is the gap. 'I have to play the part of the queen in
Macbeth.' His face is a montage of flesh turning into
stone and I hasten on, *laying* it on, my heart thrashing
round like a frightened bird. 'If you know the play, you
will know she's an evil witch, a real devil under those
jewels and the fancy robe, blood all over her hands.'

'But she's got tits and a cunt, hasn't she?' My face answers for me and he goes on, '*You* got that?' Again my
face answers and he rubs it in, 'So why does this Tony
want *you* for the part? Does he think you're one of his
pervs that ponce around like they got a marble up their
arse? Why do *you* want the part? For *this*?' Now he
kicks the parcels, so hard that the one skitters back
under the bunk. 'Only whores get paid for getting it
shoved up their holes, back or front. You wanting to be
a whore?'

'This,' I think, 'is *it*,' but raw anger seizes me before
the as-raw pain, and, for once, the anger steadies me and
I say with a calm that hacks through to him as finally as
any blade, 'Tony wants me to do the part because there
is a scene in which the Queen whispers to the audience
in the way *I* whispered in the play back there. That is
all,' and I want to add that it is all over between us –
and a lot more besides – but don't, partly because heart-
break is overwhelming me and partly because the 'That
is all' is *not* all, the knowledge of my conceit, of my
*wanting* to play the Queen, coming back to haunt me
with the horrible resilience of a strangled child.

He leaves then, wheeling hurriedly away, his face an
expressionless shield, and does not come back till swill-
and-extras time, when he collects his and I collect mine,
and I make to climb up onto my bunk, but he unmistakably and unexpectedly moves over, indicating that I
should sit in my usual place on his, and a gladness
floods me that I know I must not show, and I sit down
beside him and we eat in a silence that is more tentative
than strained. Near the end, he takes out his slice of the

morning's bread that we always save, and I take out
mine and open up the food parcel that I had left lying
in the aisle, and find in it a small jar of strawberry jam
which I then uncap and offer to him, and he takes it
with the delicate hesitancy of a grown wild cat being
tempted back into the 'normal' world, and spreads a
little of the jam on his bread and hands back the jar. So
I know, then, that I have scored a victory of a kind, but
at a cost because he now often lapses into unaccount-
able silences during which I will sometimes find him
watching me with a speculativeness that disturbs, and,
no matter how cold the nights, he no longer clambers
up into my bunk to seek and give the warmth that was
as much of the heart as of the bones, and there is a
heaviness in me because of this that nothing heals.

Right from the start, Tony insists that I rehearse in
an ankle-length shift that he has stitched together from
odd pieces of cloth for which he could find no better
use. 'So that you can get to know what it's like to wear
a robe,' he says, and I ask him what the real robe will
be like and he says that's his business, which, indeed, it
is, he being the theatre's only costumier and an irascible
and dictatorial one at that. Adept with the needle as
with the clippers and blade, he does all his own sewing
– although he says he may be taking on some casual
'seamstresses' this time round because of the many costumes that the production demands – and he is legen-
dary for never exposing his creations to either the cast's
or the public's view until the dress rehearsal, when they
are trotted out with all the fanfare of a Parisian
couturier.

Macbeth would not have had to practise in any shift, he being one of Tony's stable and, curiously enough, a civvy street cross-dresser who watches my antics with an infuriating mixture of amusement and contempt. 'Forget him,' Tony says. 'On opening night, he will be a nothing, but the goons will be eating out of your hand.' Then adds, 'That is, of course, if you do what I say.' And, truly, I try, but it is a trying by numbers, a constant warning myself not to spread my thighs when I'm sitting down, to scrunch up my buttocks when I walk like, as Danny put it, I've got a marble up my arse, to not bat my hands about as if I'm swatting flies, but to keep them supple and subtle as a thief's or a lover's – Tony's words, not mine – but *never* – and Tony mercilessly parodies his own kind – like a *queer*.

'Like what, then?' I ask.

'Like a *wife*, you ox! Like a *woman* who just *is* a woman and nothing else. And even *she* is not to be just *aped*. She it is who has always been a part of you, but you never knew it, and now you must know it and wake her and set her free, and she must move your parts and speak with your tongue, and you will look on from the sidelines like the rest of us and ask, "Is that me?" And it will be and yet it won't, and that is the miracle – the *birth* – which every actor seeks but must not *pursue* or it is lost.'

'Another great speech, maestro, but you're forgetting you're talking about the *me* in this shit,' and I tug at the shift, 'and that me knows that there is still nothing there *except* me. Two weeks now and the old cow hasn't even given a fart to show that she's alive and kicking and ready to go! For Chrissakes, Tony, why don't you use one of your guys that *already* feels like a woman and stop wasting your time with me? No matter *how* you pretty me up, I have got balls down there and know it and *like* it and nothing's going to change!'

'Now *you* come off it, Tom! If you've learnt nothing from the first play you were in, I *have*. You're a slow starter who needs a first night for everything to come together and turn you on, and how much more *powerful* that turning-on is going to be in the case of you who have never felt like a woman before than in the case of those for whom it is just another strut-around in drag? You concentrate on getting the basics of movements and lines right and the Lady will let you know on opening night that she has been growing in you all the time and is ready at last to quit that womb in you that you never knew you had.'

'Jesus, you can't half turn a guy *off*, let alone on! You going to give me a caesarean if I stall?'

'I don't think it will come to that,' he says and flashes me his small, acid grin. 'Now get to work and don't mind if I keep on at you because that is what I am not paid to do.'

Actually, Tony does not niggle me all that much. Why, I am not quite sure. Is he trying to demonstrate the fullness of his faith in me or shore up my faltering trust in myself? Whichever the case, he does not go for the jugular like he does with the rest, merely says, 'I think you know you have to do that again,' then sits in brooding silence which means I still have got it wrong, and so continues until he at last releases me with a grudging nod that holds more of reservation than acclaim. Such a seemingly preferential treatment of me does not go down well with the rest of the cast and interaction with them – and with Macbeth in particular – becomes an exercise in stoicism for which I am by nature ill-equipped, but when I complain to Tony that I am being treated like a disease, he merely grunts and turns away to sink his teeth into some other poor sod and I am wondering why the fuck I don't just walk out of here and have done?

But somehow – and I know but too well the why of it – I stick it out and, after rehearsal, hurry back to the barracks, eager for the companionship that will restore me to the real if not always more balanced world, but either he will not be there or he will be sitting listening without response to me whine on about how it went, his eyes opaque as the wrong side of a one-way glass. Never will he question me first about anything to do with the play, and when Tony takes my beard right off and cuts my hair jailbird-short in preparation for the inevitable wig, he stolidly holds up our fragment of mirror to his own unruly hairiness, then stands in the doorway of the barracks, back to me, his whole stance so expressive of separateness that it starts me throwing things around. But then I stop short, horrified, suddenly, searingly, aware that this is what a *woman* would do, that these are *her* hands, that she is surfacing even now in the way that Tony had foretold, and when he comes back and we sit down to eat, he still not openly

opposed, more tiredly resigned, I have as little to say
as he, grown afraid of the fragility of my façade.

So a new, now mutual silence settles between us,
sets hard as the long nights' ice, and I lie awake for
lengthening periods of pain, wondering if he, too, is
awake, but never sure because he was always a quiet
sleeper, not one given to snoring or thrashing about,
and wondering also, as so often before, why I don't just
walk away from it all – or why *he* doesn't just walk
away from it all – instead of leaving the corpse unbur-
ied till it rots? Are we each too stubborn to break off
before the other, he conceding me the right to ape a
woman if I want, I conceding him the right to prudishly
disapprove? – or is something deeper and finer holding
us together and we are both knowing this and not wanting to finally let it go? – or have we simply grown too
listless, with the listlessness that is the curse of all
things caged, to want to change the *status quo*?

As starkly and unsettlingly do I then also face up to
what is taking place in me. Have I let Tony – or vanity –
or both – trap me into a personality change that I will
not again be able to shake off? Fearing yet fascinated, I
let the often malevolent, often luminous beauty of the
ancient play's lines – both mine and those of the others
– echo and re-echo through my mind, Tony having
alerted me to their musicality with his seemingly offhand
yet always carefully calculated asides. Was his coaxing to
life in me this previously dormant foetus of my feminine-
ness, this shadowy, sharpening presence that is beginning to manipulate my limbs, sometimes even my as
desperately resisting tongue, equally calculating, or was

any such calculation matched by my own subliminal, never-to-be-spoken-of readiness to learn? Compellingly as an incantation, the lines possess, disintegrate me and the shadowiness rises, weaving, out of me and hovers, descends, and I start up with a cry and find that I have dreamed.

Then, as though washed up by a freak wave of time, I am standing, before the start of the dress rehearsal, swathed in the beads-and-tinsel splendour of my royal gown, Tony holding up to it his only, too-small mirror that I may view, albeit in segments, the final version of the want-to-be queen. Appalled, yet drawn, I stare at the voluptuous swelling of the padded chest, the gold-painted cardboard crown nestling in the flaming mane of the wig, the heavy-lidded, brooding eyes, the scarlet mouth's imperious slash, and think, 'Witch of my womb!' then cringe as though I had spoken the words aloud.

'You like it?' Tony demands, daring me to say, 'No,' but I nod, though my eyes are more terrified than pleased, which does not seem to upset him at all.

Then we rehearse, which is a relief, Macbeth mocking me as he is and wishing, no doubt, that *he* was wearing the gown. 'He will be a nothing,' Tony had said, 'but the goons will be eating out of your hand.' True or false? Rehearsal over, I still do not know. Certainly she has never been as near to the surface as tonight, but she is still the shadow beneath my breath's ruffling the calm, scarlet lips only now and then nibbling up to snatch a line, dimple the norm. But Tony is not fazed, is, indeed, pleased. 'Nearly there,' he says, softly punching my arm. 'Tomorrow night she will be out and

away,' which is fortifying, although I would have pre-
ferred it if he had used less apposite words.

I do not expect Danny to ask me how it went, and
he does not, so I brew up some tea and offer him a mug
which he takes. Then I crawl into my bunk, dead beat,
yet not expecting to sleep all that well, but it is snowing
again outside, the flakes drifting down like silence revealed, and it is as though a separate self in me is saying, 'I need to sleep as much as you, so *sleep*,' and I
sleep.

When I again wake, it is still snowing, but dawn is
drably about and I am expectant rather than tense and
stay that way till the drabness is twilight's and I must
go. Leaving, I look down to where Danny is fitting a
new handle of woven wire to his as makeshift a mug,
his face half-averted and remote, and, on an impulse, I
hand him the first night ticket for a friend that I had
thought I would have to give to some hopeful at the
door, and he looks at it and I bolt, not wishing to wit-
ness him tossing it aside.

Tony 'does' my face himself, hand moving swiftly,
widely, like Camel sketching, then narrowing in to the
eyes and mouth, his face absorbed as the one I have just
left, cannot forget, his tongue mercifully not burdening
me with comforting chatter or muttered last-minute advice. Almost I grow drowsy, begin to drift away into
the unreality that underlies the entire elaborate charade,
and Tony jerks up my head, saying, 'Hey!' and I become aware of the audience's roaring like a surf beyond
the dressing-room's closed door, the drawn curtains of
the stage, and at once there is a bitterness in my mouth

and my stomach heaves with a spasm of the nausea that has been lurking in me all this while like a toad under a stone.

Tony has little pity for me, though. 'Christ! Not *now*!' he moans, massaging my shoulders, neck, with impatient, admonishing hands, and my gut calms, but I am walking a thin wire now as he fusses on my wig and crown, helps me into the glittering sheath of the dress, hooking it up from behind. Only then does he allow himself to say, 'The rest is up to you now. And her.' They are the tough last words that I need and I take them with me as the overhead lights begin to flick out and I still snatch a look from between the curtains at the packed auditorium and the po-faced Krauts in the front row.

'And her,' Tony had said, and so it is. Macbeth, as Tony sees it, does not allow for a second breath. At once, it is a carnival of lights and noise, a beast ripped wide and its gut spewing out sometimes brilliant crap, sometimes jewels of imperishable truth. But she also does not permit a second breath, is ripping *me* wide from the instant of my first entrance, is a snarling tigress of malevolent cunning between my thighs. I know it is working by an almost shift of the air, a reaching out, not to me but to that which is transcending me, that is not me yet, from the beginning, has never been anything *but* this alternative according to Tom.

Tony trips the master switch and, for a moment, I, too, am thrown as he, without warning, tries out one of his sudden new ideas, tapping softly on what sounds like a home-made drum – or is he just knocking on the dressing-room door? – the beat keeping pace with me like the beating of a giant heart as I sleepwalk through the featureless dark to the front of the stage, my face and hands lit only by the single candle I am holding, its flame streaming but secure in the barely perceptible breeze. Yes, it can only be Tony, decides a remote, detached fragment of my mind as the beating stops at the exact moment of my mouth's opening to speak, a moment, that, which I prolong, facing out into the silence that is like none other because it is not the silence of desertion but of usually volatile and voluble tongues.

'The goons will be eating out of your hand', Tony had said, and that, too, is so, and I am knowing the sweetness of power and the bitterness of its encapsulated decay, but the set, with its intimations of turrets and medieval stone, is no longer enclosing me – only the timelessness of the darkness is – and there is no particular woman standing here, as there is no particular man, only an androgynous guilt that yet does not repent, would not have the deed, or the fruits of the deed, undone. 'Up now, you bitch!' I soundlessly exhort. 'Show me what you can do,' and, effortlessly, she does it again, her whisper commanding that the blood on her hands be gone, that her words be heard as, my instinct unerringly tells me, they are, eliciting the continuing silence that is the ultimate applause.

Tony is the closest to weeping – without rage, that is – that I have yet seen, hugging me without trusting himself to even say, 'I *told* you so,' his too clear partisanship ensuring that I will not be invited by the rest of the cast to the traditional first night partying with raisin booze. 'So what?' I think, coming now off my high, woodenly thanking the well-wishers who press my hand, admire the robe, but do not look at the me beneath it because I am not a resident shaman in their make-believe world, then hurry on to cluster, chattering, around the beaming Macbeth. The depression in me deepens – or is it the loneliness that refuses to be denied? – and, at last, I turn away, take off the crown and wig, wipe the goo off my face and stand, drained and reluctant to grapple with the dress.

It is then that Tony shows the true and sterling manner of himself, coming in, shouting out so that all can hear, not, 'Tom, your *boyfriend* is here!' but, 'Tom, your *mate* is here. I have told him to come and take you away from all this shit,' and leaves with a final whip-around of his tidy bum.

I turn and look at him and he looks at me and I at once know the way to go. 'Hey! You got no manners barging in when a lady's stripping down?' For a moment he is startled – is beginning to be annoyed – then he catches on and whoops it up, grinning in the way that makes me like him most, but his eyes are wet and I am thinking mine must be about the same. So I carry on, sensing that the way to go still has a way to go. 'Let me just get rid of these tits,' I say and unstuff my front, chucking the packing aside with a calculated don't-care, then again turn my back to him. 'Help me with this fucking thing,' I plead, meaning the dress, and I feel his hands shake a little as he unhooks the hooks, and the sheath shivers down and I am male again, getting goose flesh in my underwear.

We go out through the darkened auditorium, the staff already stacking the chairs so as to sweep the floor clean of the mindless litter that only humans leave, and he is standing leaning against the door's opening into the night, an improbable black cardboard hat slanting across his eyes, his mouth as shocking a scarlet slash as the again dead Queen's. 'Hello, Tom,' he says, the lips twisting in a grimace that could be either a smile or a sneer, the eyes glittering under the hat's brim. 'Welcome to the great sisterhood of creeps!'

Shock locks my tongue and it is Danny that growls, 'Get out of our way, you whore!'

Slowly, the other straightens and I see that he has already been at the raisin booze. 'Not so fast, lover,' the alien lips purr in a tone as hideously strange. 'No whore bigger than she,' then, to me, 'He giving you what you want, dear?'

Danny lashes out then with the swiftness and viciousness with which he felled Camel on the night of the bird, and seizes my arm with the passion and possessiveness of a more ancient time, hastening me along. Professional that he is, he does not have to look back to know that there will be no coming back at us, and I, too, do not have to look back, the sight of Douglas, cruciform on the floor, the grown-skeletal face smashed and bloodied and screwing up like a snivelling child's, ineffaceably imprinted on my incredulous mind.

'Christ!' is all I can say when we get back to the barracks, and again, 'Christ!' and sit, then, staring at the floor, and Danny brews us some tea and we sit sipping it, and he at last says, surprisingly resignedly rather than triumphantly, 'Now you know why I can never like this theatre shit and why I always hated that fucking cunt back there,' but I do not answer, suddenly hearing the again restive Queen whispering, 'Out damned spot!' to the blood on the hands that are also mine.

It has stopped snowing, the clouds briefly clearing and baring the steeliness of the stars, but now the temperature is plummeting as frost sugars the snow, and I crawl into my bunk and begin to uncontrollably shake, the tension that held me together breaking up and the cold slipping past it into my bones. Danny climbs in beside me then, drawing me close, saying nothing, willing the shaking to stop, and, in the morning, he is still there, quietly sleeping, but, for the first time in I don't know how long, I have an erection as pushy as a tusk, and I slip out to the nearest toilet and slyly masturbate before I piss, persuading myself that, Queen or no Queen, I am still as much of a male as ever I was.

———⟶⊷⊰⟵———

The camp's bleak surrounds deny us the traditional extravaganza of spring. The pines seem a somewhat more buoyant green, but are still no big deal and a single flowering shrub in a corner of the camp is greeted with a far keener acclaim, someone even building a circlet of stones around it to preserve it from a straying foot or vandalizing hand. In our bodies, however, the seasonal resurgence is unabashed and a certain broodiness in the air and of the eyes suggests that masturbation is on the rise as, doubtless, is the even more covert buggering which those who practise it are the quickest to condemn. There are no orgies, though, no reversions to the blindly animal couplings which the essentially lawless structure of the camp could so easily induce, the reason for this being simply – and unflatteringly – that our diet, although maintaining us at a not unhealthy level of thinness, does not arouse in us the physical equivalent of our randy dreams.

The libido stays a tricky beast, however, and Danny and I are sexually experienced enough to know this with the clarity that we should and that is wise. It is not in the nature of either of us to *discuss* a matter of this kind, but we know each other well enough by now to *sense* – or to *deduce* from small, seemingly irrelevant acts, or *abstention* from acts – what the one would so have the other know if an intangible boundary of the proprieties is not to be crossed. So when spring comes and the killer-cold is gone and there is no excuse for him to go on sleeping alongside me at night, but he only slowly relinquishes it instead of stopping it all at once, I know that he is saying, 'Look, I *liked* being with you like we were and I'm wanting you to *know* that and still feel good about it when I'm gone.' And when summer's here and the odd cautious bird sits, gaping, on the fence, and the pines seem to shiver in the heat as in a wind, and we both sleep, naked and gasping like the bird, in our bunks, and he occasionally still comes up on the pretext of having something to discuss, but now allows only his naked side to touch mine and never draws me close, I know he is saying, 'Look, what I'm *really* wanting to say is that I'm wanting to be near, but I'm knowing your body like I'm knowing mine and this is summer and the grass is dry.'

Does he mean by this that, when naked, my nakedness arouses him as his arouses me? Is he, perhaps,
thinking way back to the night in the paddock when I
took his genitals into my hand? *Does* his nakedness
wake me in a forbidden way? Involuntarily, I now, too,
think back to the night in the paddock, recall his body-
hairs' bristling against my obversely smooth skin, bolt
in a blind panic that I am powerless to control. But just
how far can I run? Relentlessly, I am forced to face up
to the nature of the relationship between us since the
play. Never closer, we are yet no longer *interchangeably*
one. He takes a certain pride in having me as his mate,
flaunts me a little as though I am a particularly snazzy
shirt or cunning knife, treats me with a subtle consider-
ateness, almost gentleness, that draws me nearer even as
it sets me apart, is, in fact, seemingly forever hooking
me *back* into that dress. That final image goads me into
wild denial, as does my reaction to the following question as to whether or not I feel *good* at being treated
with a macho possessiveness that started off with
Danny's fisting Douglas in the mouth. But, as I said,
just how far can a man run?

Douglas? Must that, too, be faced? After the shock
of watching Danny knock him flat, how had I felt?
Well, how was I *supposed* to have felt? How am I supposed to feel *now*? Jesus, I was not *married* to the guy!
Did I not make that plain enough when we broke up?
Certainly, seeing how he had changed was not the *pret-
tiest* sight of my life. Still is not. But if it is that I am
supposed to feel *guilty* about what he has *done to himself*, then no deal! If he had it in him to become a pansy

at the drop of a hat – and a black-painted cardboard hat at that – then he would have become it all the sooner had the yukky lover-boy been first on the list.

So I convince myself that I am convinced that my hands are clean, but it is easier to forget the good, the often deeply moving moments that had lit my now dead friendship for Douglas with a gracious light, than to banish the nagging thought that somewhere in the Bible it says that a man brings upon himself that which he fears, and the one thing that I fear most these days is to be involved with Douglas again. Disturbingly, there seems to be some substance to this warning because although I had only seen Douglas once in the period between the break-up and Danny hitting him after the show, I now see him nearly every day as he darts about the camp in an increasingly manic way, his face seemingly *powdered* clown-white and his eyes brilliantly restless under the brim of that ludicrous hat.

I am far from straining at the leash, therefore, when I get a message from Tony that he wants to see me straight away, my first thought being that I could be setting myself up for another awkward meeting with you know who. 'You want me to come with?' Danny asks, instantly sensing how I feel, and I laugh, barely holding back from ruffling his hair. 'No. You *start* trouble more than you stop it. And, anyway, Tony will see to it that he stays out of my way,' and I content myself with laying my hand on his shoulder as I leave. 'You watch it, hey?' he warns, leaning into my hand without seeming to. 'That slob's one heavyweight nut, if you are asking me,' and I am sure his eyes are watching me go.

At the theatre, Tony does not lead me over the stage and through the storeroom to his 'space', but takes me the long way round through the other half of the barracks where his 'staff' – Douglas surely amongst them – are lolling around like a petty elite. They stiffen, though, when we enter, then watch us pass with a tenseness to them for which I can find no cause, and I glance covertly about, checking to see if *he* really *is* there, but I do not see him and Tony, more than ever his lugubrious self, makes no reassuring asides.

Behind the cardboard wall, he seats me, makes tea, and we huddle over the ritual of the brew, and his eyes flick to me, then away, then again so, and I realize with no small surprise that Tony is *afraid*, that his fingers are straining against a trembling as they grip his mug. The silence drags and there is a silence beyond the wall that is keeping pace, and at last I ask him what is wrong, my own now uneasy hand setting my mug down with a thump that sets the tea to sloshing around.

'Yes,' he then says, his eyes now steadying on mine with the openness to which I am used. 'There *is* something wrong – so wrong that I hardly know how to deal with it and I am still asking myself if I have the *right* to share such a shittiness with you?'

'Well, you can hardly *not* tell me, now that I am here. So what is it?' and I lean to him, both wanting and not wanting to hear, moved more by curiosity than any willingness to, as he puts it, *share*.

He sighs, that very exhalation not Tony at all. 'All right. In a nutshell,' and somehow I sense the shape of it even as it looms, 'Douglas is in there,' and he jerks his head at the nearer door of the storeroom whose further door opens onto the stage. 'Both doors are locked and we have tied Douglas' hands behind his back so that he can't harm himself or anyone else.'

'You mean,' and I have no difficulty in keeping my voice calm, partly because I am not surprised and partly because I am quite callously relieved that Douglas is, after all, not prowling around, 'that he is mad?'

He nods. 'Yes. Quite mad. Does that mean nothing to you?'

'Frankly, no. Which does not mean that his *madness* leaves me cold. Madness in *any* man is not something that would leave me cold. But I am leaning – *hard* – on the "*any* man" because today – and you will have to accept this, Tony – Douglas is to me just another man.'

'I do accept that,' and his tone is emotionless as mine and I am thinking – with no small measure of craziness in myself – that we could just as well be discussing whether or not we should put more sugar in our tea. 'And I even *understand* that. But not everybody, particularly those in there,' and now he nods at the cardboard wall, 'is going to react in the same way.'

'I don't understand. What the fuck has it got to do with them?'

'A lot, my friend. One *hell* of a fucking lot! Let me explain. Last night, late, that little thread that can be strong as a silk or brittle as a hair, and that had been stretching thinner and thinner since that night when Danny knocked Douglas down, could take no more and all the bits and pieces that, when fitted together, answered to the name of "Douglas" and came when you called it and did all the little tricks that you either hated or loved, flew out like the springs and cogs of a clock you have smashed against a wall. But there was still enough sense left in the beast,' and for a moment he closes his eyes, 'to do a hatchet job on Tom Smith that – whether true or false – leaves you as splattered all over the walls as Douglas' mind. In short, you are stinking like a pole-cat out there right now, but I have agreed to keep the Krauts out of this till you have had a chance to, at least, *talk* to that poor sod,' and again he indicates the store-room door, 'and maybe – just maybe – get him back on an even keel. So that is what I am asking you to do, but I can't *force* you and if you refuse – well, then, don't blame me if nobody wants to talk to you much from now on.'

I stare at him, incredulous and enraged. 'Christ! I have never heard of anything so ridiculous in all my life! Who is it that's mad – Douglas or you and your tribe of pervs?'

I regret the insult even as I launch it, but he merely says, 'Don't think in caricatures. There are as many straights as not on my staff,' then adds with a quite gen-uine pity, 'And of course it's ridiculous. But so was Douglas' performance last night. You were the loser right from the start.'

It is then that I think of the lover-boy with the face that I would like to crush between my nails. 'What about the guy that he latched onto when I dropped him back there? Dropped him after *one whole year*, Tony, when I should have dropped him that very first day he came smarming all over me like a slug. Doesn't *that* guy also feature in this somewhere?'

'Uh-uh. That was the other way around. Douglas dropped *him* when' – and for a moment he looks vaguely uncomfortable as though he's seeing something that he had not seen before – 'when it first came out that you were going to play Lady Macbeth.'

But I miss the opening, frustration confusing me, and the silence the other side of the stacks of cardboard pressing in on me like an invisible hand, and at last I hear myself whine and am hating myself for that, 'Would *you* have liked Douglas for a mate?'

Again Tony looks at me with a pity that is real. 'As you said just now – frankly, no. But that does not change the equation between you and him.' Then he breaks me as the leaning silence cannot. 'The only equation that *is* changing, Tom, is the one between you and *me*. I never thought to see the day when you would be running around like a rat because of such a very simple thing as walking through that door.'

Almost I *hear* myself break, but still I try. 'What do you mean – a simple thing? From what you've told me, he's more likely to jump me than listen to anything I have to say. Which is not saying that I could *find* anything to say.'

'At the moment he is just sitting on a chair, staring at the wall. You would think he was OK if his hands weren't tied and his eyes would move,' and Tony looks at me with eyes as unsettling as those he describes.

Now I *do* think I see an opening that is not to be missed. 'So? How can he be bonkers the one moment

and OK the next? He's bullshitting you, man! Playing
to the gallery for sympathy and kicks. Stop listening to
his crap – slap him around a while if that will help –
and he'll be just fine!'

'It is *you* that is bullshitting *you*,' and now Tony's
voice has an edge to it that warns that his walking this
road with me is drawing to an end. 'Douglas had already slashed his left wrist with a pair of my scissors before we got to him and stopped him from finishing the
job. *That* is bullshitting, Tom?' and he waits for the
frightened fowl in me to shove its head through another
hole in the mesh, but the reality – the implacability –
of consequence has caught up with me, has clamped its
arm about my throat, and I sit, stunned and trapped as
a second Douglas on the stool, and Tony gets up and
unlocks the door, and I walk through it as to a statu-
tory death, and the door closes behind me, and the lock
clicks with the loudness of a tongue against teeth.

The light in the storeroom is not burning, so I do
not at first see him, but then my eyes adjust and suddenly he is there, rigidly upright as an extension of the
chair, his eyes acknowledging only the wall. For that I
am prepared, but not for the *totality* of the changes in
him, a completeness that so removes him from me that
any speaking to him seems an ever more meaningless
charade. Fascination heavily in me as an opiate, I stare
at him as at a crippled mute or torpid snake – it does
not matter which – seeing yet not accepting the sharply-
curving-over nose and jutting chin as they merge into
an almost saurian snout, blood-loss's blue-white pallor
overlaid with smudging mascara and other goo – for

Chrissakes why don't they clean him up or are they saving this as evidence that he is nuts? – and, most unbelievably of all, the once fussed-with, always washed brown hair become this sudden winter running wild. Only the gritted teeth seem incorruptibly the same, white and square and grinding fine some intangible abomination void of name.

What, I despairingly ask of myself, do I say to this travesty of the known, this vacated shell which I still tenaciously deny is any design of mine? Why the fuck did I allow myself to be bludgeoned into this most desperate dead end? But a residual practicality comes to my aid and I ask the first and most basic question that I must – 'Douglas, can you hear me?' – and, with an unlikeliness that makes me jump, his head bobs, though it does not even fractionally swerve. 'Christ!' I think. 'The lines are *not* down!' and am both exultant and dismayed – dismayed because I don't *want* any renewal of contact with Douglas, but also exultant in the way of a faith healer when the blind or the deaf respond to a laying on of hands.

So divided, keeping my voice emotionless and low as though I am being so directed in a play, I try again, 'That is not you sitting there. We are not friends any more and, when we broke up, I told you *why*. We were both upset and we said things we should have left unsaid' – I simply *cannot* bring myself to say 'did not mean' – 'From my side, I am sorry about that and I'm asking you to feel the same so that, together, we can stash our spooks where they belong and, even if we can't be the friends we were, at least *remember* that we were once good friends who had our good *times* along with the bad. OK?' and I wait, sweating a little from a spiritual exertion that is harder for me than a long go with a spade. But, this time, there is no bobbing of the head and I edge a step nearer, willing my words to win through: 'Come *on*, Douglas! This is not the you that I knew! The Douglas I knew was as gutsy as he had *class* and, like a rock that doesn't cat around, was always *there*. So what is this shitbag I see in that chair?' – and now anger is rousing in me and I'm wanting to be gone – 'You *proud* of the way you are now? You wanting me to *remember* you the way you are now? For Chrissakes, man, here's my hand. Take it and stop being a goddam tragedy queen!' And then I remember – a genuine shame shrivelling me small – that his hands are tied behind his back and I let my own hand swing down to where it belongs.

'Shit!' I think. 'What more can I do? How many more half-truths, whole lies, must I tell?' and I turn to knock on the door so that Tony can let me out of this small lair that reeks of sweat, cosmetics, hatred, pain.

But then the grinding teeth still and, though the head still does not turn, the mouth opens and he asks, his voice hoarse and labouring as from a terminal dissoluteness or disease, 'What do you want? Why are you snuffing round me like a dog?' For a moment I do not get it, then I do and revulsion rears in me with the bitterness of bile, and I make to break in but the oddly disembodied voice cuts me short, 'I am not deaf. I hear you even though you are so far away. I'm listening even though it's still the same old lies. All that time you were sleeping with him, you lied. And they say you are still sleeping with him. That the bunk shakes all night the way he is fucking you or you are fucking him. What difference does it make which way round?' Again I scrabble for something to say, but I am slow, shocked at how obscene 'fucking' can sound when it comes from a tongue as prissy as Douglas' used to be, and he carries on, 'So what are you doing here? Shoving your nose up my arse like you're not the same whore as me?' Frighteningly, his head at last jerks round, thrusts at me with a lizard-like speed, but the eyes are still seeing only the wall. 'He's chucked you away like the dirty washing you made *me* be?'

It is then that I find my tongue, frantically yell that which I do not believe, 'Cut the crap, Douglas! Save your play-acting for Tony and his goons! This is *me*!'

With an abruptness that overturns the chair, he is on his feet and coming to me, his steps gliding and sure, and I back up against the door, meaning to shout to Tony to let me out, then remember that the hands are tied. Irrelevantly – or is only relevancy possible in a progression that has gained a momentum of its own? – I notice that his feet are bare and the scarlet polish on the toes' nails is cracking and dulled.

'Keep away from me!' I whisper, my disgust nakedly plain, but he does not seem to hear – or, hearing, understand – only suddenly is seeing me with a slyness in his eyes.

'Untie me,' he says, turning round, and now I see that the fingernails are surfacing through the same cracking polish and the left wrist of the pathetically thin arms is strapped by as pathetic a bandage stained with drying blood.

'No!' I say, remembering the cunning in his eyes. 'Why do you want to be untied?' and think, with a bizarre hilarity bordering on hysteria, that that must be the most idiotic question ever asked.

But he sees it in quite another way. 'How can I play with you if my hands are tied?'

'What do you mean – play with me?'

'Like women play when there are no men,' and his shoulders shake with what could be a snigger or a sob, but it does not take me long to decide it's no sob.

'Get away from me, you filthy perv!' I yell, not even *trying* to be placatory now that I have seen how thin he's grown – which is a very grave mistake, he at once whirling round, butting me with his head till I reel against the door, then pushing his face into mine as for a kiss, and I again yell, as nauseated as I am enraged, and then the rage gives way to a pissing-in-the-pants little kid's fright as his teeth sink into the soft flesh of my cheek, worrying at it as would a dog's and the pain of it a flame in my brain. Then the teeth are nuzzling into my neck, seeking its throat, and my body is heaving and thrashing against the door with the mindlessness of a just slaughtered fowl, and Tony at last jerks open the door and I roll, babbling and bloodied, out and away, not once looking back, the torn loose flesh of my cheek flapping on a last shred of retaining skin.

'Fucking *bastards*!' Danny roars, rushing me off to the medical hut, hovering over me as a wisecracking orderly stitches up my cheek. 'There for life,' says the stitcher. 'Unless you shell out the bucks for a graft. But why worry? You can always tell your kids that's where they shot daddy in the war!' Then, to Danny, having fun, '*You* bite him like that?' But Danny is in no mood for fun, particularly not *that* brand of fun. 'You wanting to eat your teeth?' he retorts and is still in that mood when he later marches down to the theatre, invisible six-guns slapping his thighs, and comes back, telling me nothing, but his mood grimly quite gone.

Late that night, lights are flashing down at the theatre, Krauts are screaming orders as only Krauts chillingly can, and I do not need anyone from the rest of the darkened and tensely watching camp to tell me that they are taking Douglas away. I do not leave my bunk, my cheek beginning to throb to the beat that is peculiarly pain's, but I can hear Douglas screaming as, towards dawn, I hear myself screaming, Danny holding me down, his eyes torturedly close to mine.

⟹〭⟸

It is some way into the latter half of winter when we begin to hear nocturnal rumblings and clankings as of heavy metal being dragged across as heavy a glass. Sometimes we hear these sounds on several consecutive nights, sometimes on erratically spaced nights, and sometimes they draw tantalizingly near or remain disappointingly far, but always they come from the other side of the pines and stay in our minds for long after they have gone. Occasionally we ask the friendlier among the guards about these sounds and they then either shrug their shoulders and say it could be their tanks out on manoeuvres or they look at us with inscrutable eyes and say we are dreaming empty dreams.

Our only Russian prisoner, who looks like a mad poet with his snapping black eyes and lank scrambled hair and spends most of his time chatting to Camel who, for some reason even he seems unable to explain, is the sole 'scholar' learning Russian in the camp 'schools', says the Krauts are talking balls – or the Russian equivalent of 'balls', Camel importantly explains – these are no more their tanks than the Martians', but are, in fact, *Russian* tanks and very soon now they will be crumpling down the fences and their crews will be cutting the throats of every fucking Kraut bastard – Russian equivalents, that is – on which they can lay their hands.

All of which is, of course, very comforting, but we have as many doubts about the Russian as about the Krauts, he having told us hair-raising tales of how *he* cut Krauts' throats with naked razor-blades – where from and how? – and then expertly dribbled his way through the Kraut lines en route from his camp to ours because the food in ours was better than in his. Some of us think he may not be a Russian at all but a German spy who is feeding damaging griff back to the Kraut brass and even Camel, for once, curbs his urge to go one better in the telling of tall tales.

But, apart from lending us hope – however baseless and doomed it may be – he also tells a *pretty* as well as tall tale, describing, with so much of the imaginativeness of the poet that he seems, how these monolithic Russian tanks – 'bigger than anything we have ever dreamed' – lumber and wheel on the ice-clogged lake that is further from here than we think and is 'round and shining with a yellow-green light like it's the moon dropped down'. Whether we will one day find out the truth, is anybody's guess and, eventually, the ghostly commotion stops and does not recur and we, in turn, no longer listen, straining out through the night to the mystical – mythical? – lake and only dimly sometimes wondering if this was not, after all, the *first* of the Signs?

There are miracle days in which only those who have been in them can believe – days when the low, feathery clouds are suddenly waddling away as though some downy-arsed goose had got up from its squat, and you are seeing that the blue sky has been there all this while, only the blue has never been so near to being not and the brittleness of the air is such that you think to push your finger through it, and the sun is not really a sun, but more a burnished brass that does not even begin to soften up the snow.

It is such a day and my hands are deeply in my pockets, warming my balls, and my breath is a speech bubble with nothing in it, and I am staring through the fence with the intense vacuity that only prisoners achieve, when this Kraut comes up close on the other side and says in a struggling English that, soon now, it will be spring. I start, then grunt, in German, that the cold in my bones is telling me that nothing's changed, and he asks, surprised, where I learnt German, and I say, 'Here,' and then he asks, 'Why?' and I shrug, not daring too heavy a foray into a still only half-mastered tongue.

But my shrug does not put him off. As plainly

pleased as he is surprised, he flatters me by dropping the English, and I battle to understand as he tells me with a clear longing of his wife and child, and where he comes from and where he hopes to soon again be. But then somebody shouts from a sentry box and he readjusts his rifle strap as he repeats that soon now it will be spring – 'already its heart beats under the snow' – then leaves, only looking back once to whisperingly add, his eyes strangely and entreatingly sad, 'For *you* – this spring.'

For a long while I stare at where a corner of the fence axed him from my view, toying with a hesitant hopefulness, not daring to fully engage it, wondering if I have been shown a Sign less fanciful than the tanks on a lake that is like a 'moon dropped down?'

There is nothing ambiguous about what happens next. It brooks no denigration or denial, is, like the Apocalypse, overwhelmingly what it is. It is not as explosive, though, as the Apocalypse, nor as brutally seminal as the Big Bang. On the contrary, the first intimations of it are subliminal – a droning on the far perimeters of sense that is as irritating and inescapable as an insect circling a high light in a windowless room. Slowly, relentlessly, the droning swells, narrows in, is eventually no longer a resonance more of the mind than in the ear, but a troubling of the air itself, a vibration that sets a single yet clinching speck of dust to a settling on the back of my hand.

We go out then, stand in our thousands, looking round, seeing only the usual monotonousness that we see even when we close our eyes. But the droning does not let up, grows louder, is at last so loud that we start shouting in order to be heard. 'What *is* it?' we ask each other, at first a little foolishly, expecting the rational explanation that will send us, laughing, away. But only bafflement answers bafflement and we begin to feel estranged and afraid, to shiver a little in another of the rare clear winter days.

Then someone screams, 'There! There!', swinging an arm up at the sky directly over our heads, his eyes huge and exalted as though he witnessed the heavens opening and childhood's angels descending in a swirl of robes and wings. 'Christ Almighty!' I whisper with more of reverence than rote, my head flung back till my neck cricks as I watch the vast armada of planes passing seemingly slowly on their way to whatever culmination they seek. Dropsical with death, the bombers forge with a blind obduracy through the thin, yielding tides of the air, and the fighters flit about them with the silver glitter of gnats and someone is shrieking, voice a eunuch's with delight, 'Watch those babies *go!*' But one of the Krauts sneers that these are *their* planes, not ours, but we have already seen that the machine guns in the sentry boxes have swivelled skywards even though the planes are out of range, and when a lone battery somewhere out on the plains opens up, its guns sounding like popping corks in the overriding roar of the planes and the shells exploding humiliatingly far short, we whoop some more and the guard turns away and shambles off, ageing as he goes. Only then do I realize that Danny is gripping my arm as tightly as any tourniquet, and I turn around, but my arm could be a wooden post for all he knows and tears are streaming down his face with the shamelessness of water gushing from a stone.

Inevitably reaction sets in, but, like an old love, the original euphoria never quite goes away. We are still soldier enough to know the meaning of mastery of the skies and the Kraut colossus, that straddled us with so casual a contempt, is at a stroke the tumbled idol and the sunken fables of our own bloods and soils are rising up again as from an enchanted sea. Put less elegantly, we are the stabled horses, still fetlock-deep in straw and our own dung, but knowing now that soon the doors will open and we be let out to gallop, tails up and knotted and arses farting at the wind.

All too soon comes the testing of this new spiritedness, a testing that we know but too well and that is all the more agonizing for its being known. The Red Cross parcels that, under the Krauts, had been so unfailingly distributed that we had come to regard them as a right rather than a gift – sometimes even (after the fashion of the Israelites and the manna from God) criticizing what they held – summarily stop. As summarily are the despised Kraut rations then reduced – sometimes even halved – and the last and the surest Sign of a second tottering of our haven of cards is prowling the barracks with slavering jaws, staring over a bunk's edge with luminous eyes.

But, this time, we hold firm, particularly when the still lingering vision of the heavenly armada is reinforced by rumours too strong to be only rumours that our tottering is the *Krauts'* tottering and the very shuddering of our Eden is a reason for hope. Fired by a bonhomie born of an incipient nostalgia for what will one day be what *was*, we renew our contact with the no longer dour staff (does his bête noire of Douglas briefly haunt me there?), and, incredibly, Camel comes to visit us, clearly throttling back his more irreverent self and proffering Danny his hand as though the hand he is seeking never socked him in the teeth. I tense when I see that, but Danny takes his hand, albeit a little stiffly, and Camel and I carry the conversation until Danny, even more astonishingly, asks Camel if he still paints, and Camel nods and Danny says he would like to have a painting of himself to give his wife when he gets home, and Camel gapes, clearly at a loss for words, then, unable to any longer repress his truer self, asks, 'With or without clothes?' and I close my eyes in anticipation of that ever eager fist, but Danny says, in a tone as neutral as the Kraut soup, 'With clothes,' and I open my eyes to see that Camel is grinning and Danny is grinning back, leaving me the odd man out, but who cares?

The current about the camp, as within the camp itself, is running too swiftly now for that painting ever to be done, but a breach is healed and, on one of his increasingly frequent visits, Camel suggests that we go with him to visit Tony, and I instinctively touch the scar on my cheek and, as instinctively, glance at Danny, neither of us having even mentioned Tony's name since the mauling of me in that unforgettably foetid little room. But Danny says, 'OK. Tony's all right,' which is the first indication that he has ever given me that the confrontation between him and Tony on that climactic day must have been more complex than I supposed.

There is a silence, but more of surprise than hostility, as we pass through to Tony's 'space'. He greets us as though we have never been away, his eyes only briefly fleeing as we first come in, but he does not offer us tea, it being not to be *had* any more and all stalls (as with every other 'business', including ours) closed down in a repeat of the 'crash' of two years before. But there is no repeat of his apathy of then and an emotion close to true affection seizes me as I watch the now almost savagely emaciated face glow with an ardour worthy of a less ephemeral cause than shunting actors around on a stage.

'It will be our swan song,' he enthuses, 'the most difficult thing I have ever done! You have this bloke who's going to the dogs with booze and women and what have you in a bungalow somewhere in Africa where there's lots of greenery coiling round the walls and leopards coughing in the wings. He deals in diamonds and slaves which means — naturally — that he is a white bounder whose rich Brit dad has kicked him out of the house with enough of a remittance a month to shut his mouth and keep him a continent away. Now that sounds like a load of corn and it *is*, but there's also this young native girl who's shacked up with him and *she's* the one that makes this play the one I want to do before our deliverers come to drag me out of here!'

'Who's going to play the part of the girl?' I dare to ask, curiosity overcoming caution as I realize the magnitude of the task Tony is setting not only the actor but himself.

'*Present* tense, Tom, not future. Not knowing how

much time we have left, I have speeded up rehearsals to the point where I lie awake at night picturing the balls-up there is going to be on opening night.'

'Which is – ?' Camel prompts.

'In a week's time,' and Camel says, 'Christ!' and Tony turns to me again and says, 'You don't know him, Tom. Not your sort. Nor, for that matter, mine. But, when it comes to plays, I'm looking for *actors*, not friends, and he is *good*.'

'What does this creep do to the girl?' Danny cuts in and, although his tone seems normal enough, I'm wishing we were somewhere else, the conversation veering now towards perilous ground.

'Give him one guess,' Camel says, making it worse, and I making it worse still as Camel's usual dry lasciviousness jerks a laugh out of me that is more nerves than mirth.

'Shut up, Camel!' and Tony seems genuinely annoyed, then turns and lays his hand on Danny's knee, which does not flinch. 'I will send you each a ticket for opening night. Use it or throw it away. It is your choice. But be sure of one thing and that is that I would never have offered this part to Tom, not only because he would have turned it down, but because it would have offended you who are his mate and whom I too respect, as I am sure you are knowing by now.'

Back at the barracks, I look at Danny with real concern. 'You getting to *like* gays?'

'Nah. Why do you ask?'

'Well, you and Tony seem to be doing just fine, and you are not exactly kicking Camel in the face, and you did not say you are *not* going to see this play which is going to be a pretty rough man-loves-man affair, if you are asking me.'

'You getting jealous?' Danny taunts, having fun, and though I *know* he is having fun, the bizarreness of such banter fazes me and I stare at him, at a loss for a reply. He relents, then, punching my arm. 'Hey! I'm just bulling you, man! But Tony *is* all right. He's got savvy and a heart and he's not all the time thinking about that one thing. If they were all like him, I reckon I could learn to live and let live. *Camel* I'm not so sure about, but he hasn't bothered me yet and I'm thinking he won't after what I gave him back there. About the play? Well, you heard what Tony said. "Use it or tear it up." I'll see how I feel when the time comes.'

Tony sends us our tickets the next day, the bearer being a youth who looks like one of Tony's 'straights', but they say you never can tell. I hand Danny one of the tickets and he looks at it, then hands it back to me, saying, 'Keep it with yours,' he having no patience when it comes to matters such as this, and I stash the tickets in the hulk's now getting very tattered kitbag. 'Did the poor bastard ever get buried?' I belatedly wonder, rolling the bag back under Danny's bunk, a small sadness skittering through me like a dead leaf in a wind.

Danny clams up that following week, aping our shrunken – and still shrinking – stomachs which I have come to picture as sly, voracious louts that snap up every least scrap of food, then shovel it into our systems with nothing left over for a turd. Occasionally and un-controllably, though, they *do* let off vast farts that reek of the turnip soup we so loathe but dare not any longer refuse. At times, masochistically driven, I stare into our fragment of mirror and flinch at the cadaver that stares back at me, or I feel my hipbones and shudder at their jutting and am almost grateful that it is too cold to strip down and the Krauts are to be thanked that their frequent herding us into the delousing chamber is preserving us from the peculiarly Ite pestilence of lice.

Danny is not, however, *sullen* as are our stomachs – is, I sense, merely worrying with his usual tenacity at a problem which concerns only himself, but which he will eventually resolve and then share, and I am only surprised at what the problem was when, on the morning of the show, he looks at me with faintly challenging eyes and says, 'We can go,' and I know that he is knowing that I will not be asking, 'Where?' What I am asking *myself* is why did he seemingly so agonize over a matter which he originally dismissed with the words, 'I'll see how I feel when the time comes'? But I am none the less selfishly pleased by his decision because, from the start, I have *wanted* to go to the show, partly because I have come to love the stage and partly because it will take my mind off my stomach for an hour or two. However, I am still – and hardly less selfishly so – concerned that the *nature* of the play will revive Danny's old intolerance of gays and disrupt the present pleasant *status quo*.

I could, of course, have gone on my own, but would *not* have, which – considering the moodiness that would have ensued – is also not as selfless as it sounds, and I am being at my *most* selfish when I say,

'OK, but remember I warned you that you might not like the play.'

'Maybe I'm going because it *is* what it is,' and my astonishment shows and he grins a little grimly as he adds, 'No, it's not quite *that* simple, mate. *Nothing* is that simple. I thought this place would have taught *you* that before it taught it to me,' but he does not explain further, instead turns his back to me as though signalling that the subject is closed, then stretches his arms up straight and yawns, but I'm thinking that the yawn has a stagy sound. Then he drops his arms again and, his back still to me, asks, his tone carefully offhand, 'You wanking much these days?'

It is as though he has fisted me in the gut, we – despite our otherwise closeness – never having discussed anything *this* personal before, but I try not to rock the boat too hard, 'Who says I'm wanking at all?' and I'm hating the coyness of the question even as it slips out of me beyond recall.

His shoulders shake, but with as much discomfort as mirth, 'Come off it, mate! You a girl? I thought we were mates enough to talk about *anything* between ourselves. And, anyway, I'm not fishing around just for fun. I've got something big on my mind.'

'Well, no,' I confess, embarrassment still moving in me like a mess of ants. 'Not for a long time, if you must know. I suppose it's the shit food.'

'Same with me,' he grunts. 'Don't know when last.'

'So what's the problem? Why are you pitching me this crap?'

For answer, he gropes under his palliasse, takes out

a sheaf of letters, selects one and passes it to me, his eyes still not meeting mine. 'Read,' he says and goes to stand in the barracks door, staring out into the inexhaustibly falling snow.

The letter is from his wife, the handwriting girlishly fine, the date four months earlier than the camp censor's date of barely a fortnight ago. It teems with crudely sloppy sentiment, is concerned only with herself, is awakening in me a dark resentment that has a truer name that I flee. The concluding words leap out at me from the page, 'Pray to Jesus, dear, that this war will soon be over. I am only human, you know. I am a woman and I'm needing my man!'

Decisively, I refold the letter, return it to its envelope, toss it onto Danny's bunk, and he comes over and I say, trying for humour, but the tightness in me still plainly to be heard, 'Ja, looks like you got to work overtime when you get home!'

He does not at first reply to that. Looking at me levelly, seriously, he instead says, 'I understand how you feel. I would feel the same if − ' and he nods at the letter, then lets the sentence hang. 'Nah, that's shit. I *am* feeling the same. Right or wrong, it will be hard when the time comes.' Then he narrows in to land, 'Why am I showing you that letter? Don't you see? It's like you said. Like *she's* saying,' again he indicates the letter. 'These women of ours − there must be *some* bint waiting for you too, man! − if they are not having it off with somebody else − and I can't see *my* missus doing a thing like that, not with my *mum* there, that's for sure! − they will be so hungry for it when we get back that they will be wanting us to give it to them before we even close the door, and here you are saying – and *I* am saying – that we can't even get it up any more, haven't even been *wanting* to wank for we don't know how long! Jesus! Every time I read that letter and feel this dead meat between my legs, I'm wanting to go any-where except home!' He stops, breathing hard, rubs a small moisture from his hands, his eyes wider than I have ever seen them and more than a little mad. Then, almost pleadingly, 'Do you think they will understand what it was *like* here, that we have been only half-way men most of the time? Do you think they will be *pa-tient*, will believe us when we tell them we have grown to be just plain *scared*?'

I stare at him, at a loss what to say. What can I *possi-bly* say? What inane advice can I proffer when – give or take a year or so – we are the same age and *he* the mar-ried man? Feebly I repeat what I said about the food, as-suring him that we will be fine again when we are fed, but, deep down, fearing that that, too, is a load of crap, that we are not likely to be in any very much better shape when they again dump us on doorsteps we hardly any longer know. Then I remember my mother – clair-voyant and ferocious, raging at my father for what she had caught him doing to me, but then standing by him, trying to understand him, to help him, even though they never again shared the same bed – and I say, a little more authority in me now, 'Women are not like us. We can't judge them by what *we* are. They are also *mothers*, you know, and sometimes we are less their men than their kids whom they cannot bring themselves to kick

in the teeth even though we deserve to have our cocks
cut off with a blunt knife. So steady up, mate. You are
married to a nice Brit girl, not to a –' and for a moment
I hesitate, and then it comes to me and I say it right –
'Lady Macbeth', and he begins a slow grin, then touches
my arm and stashes the letter back under the palliasse
and says he's going out for a piss.

So we go to the show, shivering under a briefly
cleared sky, an over-the-snow wind smashing into our
faces like shattering glass. Rumours of the show's eroti-
cism have been deliberately floated and hungrily heard
and it is plain that every first-night ticket has been pre-
sented at the door. Only the Kraut brass are conspicu-
ously not there and there is an immediate new rash of
rumours that peace is about to be/has been/has long
since been declared and the Kommandant has been
summoned to hand over whatever Kommandants hand
over at the changing of the guard.

The play itself is even worse than Tony had warned
and I find myself unable to beat back the yawns, but
Danny sits staring at the stage with a massive remote-
ness that makes him seem twice his size. The actors are
indeed, as Tony had feared, under-rehearsed and I find
myself waiting in mounting tension for the prompt's
next too loud intervention from the wings. The actors
*are* doing their best, though, their mouths bleeding
from their wrestling with the playwright's barbed wire
lines, and the 'native girl' is all that Tony enthused 'she'
was – sensuous yet rawly innocent and the whole stun-
ningly believable under a miracle of make-up that has
the whistles shrilling each time an entrance is made.

Our seats are near the stage and I study this illusion
of a woman from every angle, but – from the sinuous-
ness of the hands to the pouting of the mouth and the
lilting of the tidy buttocks – there is no flaw. Indeed,
there is *more* – a *personality* that is so wholly feminine,
so little put on, that I realize it must be the actor's own
covert personality now orgasmically set free.

The anticipated sex scene is as I had foreseen. The remittance man, in shorts and vest – this is Africa where
the playwright thinks it's never cold and everyone
sleeps in the raw – is inviting the 'girl' to a canoodling
and she dressed only in a sarong – what else? – and a
strip of flowered material she has knotted across the si-
mulated breasts. But she keeps on shaking her head,
and at last he rips the sarong from her and, momentarily, it is bared – the ultimate illusion of a vagina – the
penis twisted back and somehow secured between the
thighs and the splayed testicles suggesting the soft cush-
ioning of a cunt. 'Jesus!' I involuntarily whisper, 'what
if the poor sod wants to piss?' but Danny does not hear
me, as massively intent now as he was massively aloof,
and the remittance character flings the girl across a
table – conveniently placed – and, back to us, drops his
shorts and begins to 'rape' the girl, his buttocks thrusting in his finest stab at acting so far. Oddly, there are no
catcalls or whistlings throughout this scene and the almost respectful silence continues till, in the end, the girl
– how else? – stabs the guy and there is gore all around
in the manner of Tony's Macbeth', and the curtain falls
and there is a standing ovation and curtain calls, during
the last of which the camp's one-time biggest gambler

whisks the 'girl' away, she turning out to be his real life moll.

We slosh back to the barracks through the snow, the wind even sharper than when we came, and I glance aside at Danny walking silently beside me, but the little I can see of his face tells me nothing at all and I begin to fear that I have a problem on my hands. 'Well, I *did* warn you,' I defensively begin, but he says, 'It's OK,' as though accepting an apology from me and wriggles his chin deeper into his scarf.

'Yes – well – it shouldn't worry you and me all that much, this guy doing it to another guy. After all, we had it done to us as kids, so it's nothing new.'

For a moment he looks at me in bewilderment, then he seems to remember and says, 'Oh, *that*,' and says nothing more, which could be odd, but not more so than *my* relatively phlegmatic witnessing of that which once had me crying out in dreams. Has there been a catharsis somewhere along the line?

So we walk on in a silence that again grows too long and again I try: 'She was the best of the lot, though I never forgot that the "she" was a "he".'

Startlingly, he explodes, 'She should have carved the bastard up slow! Not just stick him once dead!' and I realize that *he* is remembering a 'she', not a 'he', and it is the 'she' that is walking beside him through the fake African sun en route to his bunk, and an emotion that refuses to be acknowledged as anything but jealousy stirs in me like a viper coming out of sleep.

'It was only a show!' I laugh, spite's forked tongue flickering under the laugh, and he looks at me with something close to distaste and refuses to again be drawn.

At the barracks, we ready ourselves for bed, which means kicking off the clogs from our double-socked feet, and I climb into my bunk and wait for him to follow, this being too cold a night for sleeping alone, but then I hear him rooting around in his own bunk and alarm seizes me and I ask, anxiety thinning my voice, 'You not coming up?' He does not answer, lies still, listening, and at last I plead, 'Come *on*, Danny! It's fucking cold up here!' and he grunts, 'All right,' and comes up then, but turning his back to me so that we lie back-to-back, he seeming to fall at once asleep but I lying a while, disgruntled and more than a little hurt.

I wake and he's fidgeting beside me as though he's got ants or a rash, and I'm about to ask him what's wrong, when I hear him breathing in a way that I know but too well. The rhythmic movements of his buttocks are no less a giveaway and I'm shouting to myself, 'The bastard's wanking! That's why he wanted to sleep alone!' and I go on listening, my bitterness spawning more bitterness as *he* goes on – as I pettishly put it – 'fucking that whore!' But then I realize that his grappling with himself is carrying on inordinately long, that he is stopping ever more frequently and starting up again ever more desperately and his breath is verging on a muted groan. 'He can't come,' I decide. 'He's got it up like he said he couldn't and now he can't come,' and, when he again pauses, I reach out as though compelled by a force outside of myself – is it compassion or simply triumphalism that I am about to do for him what the phantom woman never can? – and take his penis into my hand, gently sliding it in and out of the curve of my palm, sometimes rubbing its tip between my finger and thumb as so many lusting women have done for me in my once upon a time, and, at first, he resists, his back stiffening, iron and long, but then his buttocks begin to move to the rhythm of my hand, and I quicken the play and he quickens the response and, at last, he gathers himself and a small sad fluid is wetting my skin. I keep on a little, hoping for more, but hunger has taken its toll and I loose the already retracting penis and close my palm over the pitiful yield that, somehow, does not disgust me as much as would my own.

In the morning, I wake first, my hand still clenched and my own thighs now wet from an unremembered dream, and I go out to the taps and wash myself as best I can without stripping down, and, when I get back to the bunks, Danny is also up, but his eyes are not meeting mine and his whistling is brash and loud as some little kid just come back from a mischief that could earn him the belt. 'What now?' I think, embarrassed as he. 'How do we get back to where we were?' and the swill comes and we eat it, and we are talking to each other, but looking past each other like we've both gone cross-eyed overnight. And then we are sitting staring into our empty dixies as though we have never before seen their bottoms bared of swill and I say to myself, 'Sod this!' and tackle the issue head-on. 'You feeling better now?' I ask, matter-of-factly as though he's had a headache and I'm hoping the pill helped, and for the first time we look at each other squarely and he blurts out, 'Why did you do it?' and I'm ready for that and grin, forcing him to hesitantly grin back, 'Well, I could tell you something fancy like it was for friendship's sake, but the truth is it looked like you were going to be at it all night and I wanted some sleep, so I gave you a push,' and his grin widens and, unusually for him, he takes my dixie and goes to wash it together with his under the taps.

Back, he fusses around in his bunk, then asks, carefully casually, not looking round, 'Did I come all right?'

'Just about blew my hand off,' I say, feeling expansive, knowing I have beaten the phantom woman this time round, and he laughs and I breathe out, slowly and long, feeling my flesh cringe at the closeness of my skidding round the bend.

Tony doesn't quite make it with his show. It is only about a quarter of the way through its projected run of a month when the Krauts warn us that we have four days in which to ready ourselves for a march to a new camp in the far south. They quote 'tactical redeployment of prisoners' as the reason for this, but we still remember our own armies' tricky jargon when it comes to not saying what dare not be said, and we immediately pounce on 'tactical' and 'redeployment' as proof positive that the Krauts are shitting in their pants. The *absolute* clincher, of course, is that we are to '*march*' – 'They haven't even got *transport* any more!' somebody gloats – and we go around jeering at the guards and the better of them stare at us with pitying eyes that should have warned but don't.

Convinced that we will not be marching to any new camp, but to some airport/harbour/station where bands will be playing and the requisite planes/ships/trains waiting to carry us back to our lost loves and the sweeter Edens that this one so mockingly apes, we embark on an orgy of chucking-out or using-up, right down to the last of the raisin wine which the cherishers of it summarily gulp, then cast up again as the outraged bellies rebel. Sombrely in step, the Krauts trundle barrowloads of files and other administrative bumf from the main office block to a wooden shed closer to the gates, where they stash them with an insane meticulousness before drenching the shed with petrol and setting it alight. It goes up in a great gush of flame that would delight any child and we, grown that child again, foolishly acclaim, waltzing one another round, yelling as at a celebration of a setting-free – 'Or an expunging,' comes the sobering thought as I watch our names, heights, colours of eyes, shrivel into the nothingness that we now are.

Through what quirk of kindness – or is it subtle sadism? – do the Krauts spare our still-to-be-censored letters, dumping ten potato sacks of them on our side of the fence, inviting us to do with them what we will? The more dutiful amongst us drag the sacks out of the snow into the theatre and empty them onto the auditorium floor, but there is no scramble for them, many of us, Danny included, so confident that they are going home that they could not be bothered pawing over letters whose news is probably now as irrelevant as it is old.

Those that do still care are to be seen picking over the increasingly muddied letters like crows picking bits out of the cadavers of murdered men, and Camel is one of them and, gaunt and more than ever lurching like his irritable namesake, comes to where Danny and I are sitting on Danny's bunk and nibbling at the last of our boiled potatoes and, handing Danny a letter, says, 'Hey, you nearly missed out on this one!' and Danny thanks him and he says, 'Not so fast. Letters are sneaky shits. I never trust the fuckers before I know what it is that they have to say,' and shambles off again, and Danny looks at the letter and says, 'From my mum,' then laughs as he adds, 'Can't be much in there I still want to hear, me going to surprise her any day now,' and he lays the letter down beside him and finishes his potato before he again takes it up, fumbles open the envelope and starts to read.

I watch him and it is like watching one of those movies where this character drinks some shit or other and begins to change – but slowly – so slowly that you hardly realize it till there he's sitting looking at you like nobody you have ever seen or known. 'What is it, Danny?' I ask, and he must be hearing me because he lifts that alien face and stares at me, but his eyes are wholly blind. 'What *is* it, man?' I again ask, the concern in my tone veering now towards fear, and I reach out my hand to touch him, to return him from where he is now, but he strikes my hand aside and, surging to his feet, eyes still staring at his private rage, makes to go, and again I put out my hand, but to restrain him now, and his fist crashes between my eyes, flinging me against the bunks, and the barracks, not understanding, is roaring at us to 'cut out that crap' and, when I again can see, he is gone and only the letter, crumpled and flung to the floor, is evidencing that this is for real.

Imagining all eyes are on me, I slink out and hold the cold snow to my aching face, convinced that my eyes are already beginning to puff shut, then go back and the letter is crackling under my feet, and I pick it up and unfold it, the hurt and bewilderment in me over-powering any guilt I might otherwise have felt. Dated three months later than the letter from his wife which he allowed me to read, this is a boring recital of unfami-liar and mundane events which I skim through in search of the serpent in the brush and, near the end, there it is. 'Son,' she says, 'I have to tell you this, but *how*? Night after night, I have lain awake, *wondering* how, and I have decided that I must just tell you all at once, the way I used to give you your medicine when you were still small and had the 'flu. Son, Bessie's gone. Gone off with another man. Says she can't take it any more. I would like to lie to you and tell you that that is the *whole* of this thing because that would save you a little pain *now*. But you will find out more when you come home and be hurt all over again, so know now, and pray to the Good Lord to give you the strength to hold on, that she went with him carrying his child. She is nothing but a whore, son, and you must not − ' but now shame at my prying *does* stir in me and I crumple the letter up again, but, this time, lay it on his bunk, not wishing anybody to pick it up from the floor as did I and so be privy to his pain.

It is snowing again and I am wondering where he is
and, knowing him, worrying that he will do something
rash. So I walk the length of our barracks, but he is not
to be seen, and I look through windows at Tony and
Camel and staff, but they are alone, and I walk all the
way round the camp, but see only guards slapping their
sides, and, the whole time, thoughts are circling in my
mind like flies flocking to a still fresh turd. So *I* am
privy to his pain, but do I *share* in it? – and I insist that
I do, am *certain* that I do, it being monstrously impossible for me to react in any other way. But do I share in
his grief at his having been betrayed by his *wife*; do I,
like him, wish with a frantic heart that the perfidious
Bessie had been less dismissive of her churchly vows?
'Jesus!' I protest – to what? 'She was not *my* wife!' and
uncomfortably know that my clumsy side step has not
freed me from the snare.

Finally, I check on all the toilets, but none of the
buttocks are his, and I stand outside the last toilet, pain
from the blow growing restless as a trapped animal in
my skull and my anxiety competing with irritation as
the chill settles ever more solidly in my bones, and, at
last, a logic perfidious as Bessie persuades me that I
could walk about the camp all night and remain one
step behind wherever Danny happens to be. 'What
more *can* I do?' I whine and my devil, weaving, comes
in through my pain-weakened defences and, with the
deadly reasonableness that is his, warns that Danny is
quite capable of bashing me again if I don't let up and
leave him alone.

So I do just that and head for our barracks, a last

shred of guilt trailing me like a nagging child, and he is standing outside the door, watching me come, and I stop, uncertain what to do – uncertain of what *he* is going to do – and he comes to me, shaking his head as I move back a step, and touches my wincing, now all-but-shut eyes with hesitant hands, then burrows his face into my neck and begins to weep, soundlessly, the sobs racking him till I'm thinking they will tear him in two.

And I am making shushing noises now as though that child has caught up with me, and he is saying, over and over again, his voice disbelieving and wild, 'Christ! what have I done? Oh Jesus Christ! What have I *done?*' and, most satisfyingly of all, 'That bitch! That *fucking* bitch!' and it is no longer so difficult for me to admit that I *am* glad that Bessie has turned out to be a bitch and a whore.

I don't sleep very well that night, he not helping much with his frequent visits to the taps to wet his ragged and no longer so clean towel with water so's he can lay it like a compress over my eyes, but I suffer this because it is yielding me as much of pleasure as the reverse and I know that it is helping him to grapple with his own hurt that is still hugely there under the tissue of his rage. My eyes are, indeed, far closer to recovering than his heart – *is* there any curing of the heart? – when we at last line up outside the gates and the guards, again missing the two guns, hastily rifle through our kits, then issue us with extra rations and – in a joyous repeat of two years back – a sudden Red Cross parcel each.

Only the odd flake is still falling and the snow on

the road leading out is turning to slush under the shuffle and stamp of the feet waiting for the order to march,
and, Danny woodenly at my side, I look back at the
desolation that we leave. Acres of paper and empty tins,
palliasses, charred and fouled, uncounted hosts of clogs
– how can one march in clogs? – only the precious
army boots will do for this last mile – a greatcoat, that
could still have been worn, senselessly sprawled as a
dead man – are these to be our sole bequests to those
who follow after in search of the courage and greatness
that raised us to the heights we have never seen?

Almost guiltily, I again turn my back to the bitter
Eden that we are for the second time abandoning, that
housed us with however much of harshness and that we
now cast aside as did the lusting Bessie this sombre re-
ject at my side. Disbelievingly I watch as the fallen angels of the guards, those once Watchers at the Gates,
busy themselves with the pettinesses of our kits, and
Danny suddenly, urgently, whispers, 'Don't look to
your right!' but of course I do and my hair seems to rise
up straight as a scalded cat's as I see that Douglas is staring at me through a window small and barred as a cell's.
'Irrenhaus' states a sign on the wall in which the window is set, but this I notice only subliminally, my eyes
locked with Douglas' as in a horrifying embrace. 'Hello
there!' he calls, his voice coy as a girl's and soaring with
an impossible clarity above the hubbub all around, but
now I wrench my eyes away and pretend I do not hear,
but he persists and a quick glance sickens me with the
sight of his now coquettishly fluttering hand. 'Fuck off!'
I at last yell, ignoring Danny's restraining grip on my

arm, the whole of me shuddering with nausea and rage, and Douglas seems able to hear me as clearly as I am hearing him because he at once unleashes a torrent of spectacular abuse.

Do they, too, hear — these two SS men strutting past with their peaked black caps with the death's-head badge and the high black boots made for wading through shit or blood? Or were they bound for the madhouse anyway, weapons the one-digit extensions of their hands? Whichever, they go round to the rear of the asylum's concrete cube, there being no door opening onto the road, and at once there is a boiling as of bodies trying to escape through the facing window's bars, and a shrieking that stills us as though a Biblical curse had struck us into figures of salt or stone. Then the shots come, and continue till the shrieking stops, but there is one who is still alive, and he slips past the too slowly wheeling guns and is bolting out from behind the cell and into us, his hair flaring like his flaring eyes, and we are all making way for him, but more in a fearing for our own lives than from any nobler urge, and they pump him full of bullets as he hurtles into the camp fence and claws, despairingly, at it and lies there, his arms flung wide and his eyes amazed that his scraggy body should still be yielding up so much of blood.

They drag him then, back across the road to the asylum, and fling him like a sack against its wall, and even our guards stay silent as ourselves, as the no doubt blood-drenched madhouse from whose window — as from every other window — Douglas' tormented image has forever been expunged.

Then the order comes to move and we move, but pacing now as mourners do, the true nature of what we face at last starkly revealed.

⟶⟩●⟨⟵

We do not pass through any further ruined cities, my German coming in useful as I hear our guards bickering amongst themselves that even that one instance was a mistake, that it was never meant that we should see one of their cities in that state. So now we meander southwards along mainly farm roads or tiny villages' cobbled lanes, and sometimes we even find ourselves struggling, single file, along fences between homesteads and the farmers' wives and children are watching us from behind the windows' pretty curtains with terror and despair – and only the very occasional hatred – plainly in their eyes. 'A beaten people,' I mumble to Danny, but he only grunts, seeing only the snow.

Bemused though we are by the anguish of the flesh as of the mind – I still haunted by the horror of Douglas' death and Danny walking skewed as men will after the loss of a limb that is the loss of a wife – we none the less dimly sense that we are lurching from winter into spring. The clouds more frequently yield to the still temperate but strengthening sun, there is a shyness to the snowfalls that foreshadows their end and, once, one of the guards – who has discovered I understand Kraut and now seems to have as little to eat as ourselves – excitedly points to a flower pushing up through the shallower snow and says, 'Schneeglöckchen!' with an awe and a delight that only aggravates my misery and draws from me not even a try for his joy.

But Danny and I do sometimes whisper to each
other of spring, confess to each other – and to ourselves
– that we are sliding into a submissiveness that invites
death while all else is reaching for birth and vow, then,
to cling – cling even beyond our strength – to the thin
thread of the breath that is our life. But there is still so
much of snow, still the undeclared distance we must go,
the ever faster ebbing of our strength and will as the
powerhouses of our bellies shut down and even intelligence in its ivory tower falters, hearing madness sneaking up the stairs.

So we are sleepstaggering along this track skirting a
forest of trees we will never name, the snow on either
hand liquidizing into a slow slush like rotting flesh, and
dusk is drawing in and we are listening for the command to stop and slump down into the deeper sleep
that sometimes settles into the final foetus that is
death. But they head us off under the trees where the
snow still lies shin-deep, unbroken and spite-white, and
we go on stumbling down a trail marked only by the
spacing of the trees, grumbling without rage, driven by
guards whose faces are as honed by the long march,
long walking alone, mouths set in a rictus of mechanical
command.

At last they shout, 'Stop!' and we collapse, but they
order us up again and we see them then, pacing down
the line, fed and to be feared in their black caps, black
boots, black gloves for murderous hands, faces fish-
belly-pale, blue eyes blazing out of the nothingness beyond. There are only four of them but their presence is
a horde's, and the guards shuffle round them, saluting

them with flaccid arms, inaudible 'Heils!' and they expostulate, threaten, rage, their voices rising to the porcine screams of their totem and god, but they are too distant for me to hear what they say.

Then, unbelievably, we are ordered on, but now at an increased and increasing pace, till at last we are almost running, weaving, stumbling, sometimes smashing into trees, sometimes falling as the snow drags us down. Some stagger up again, some lie where they fall, and a so long supine rebelliousness begins to stir, but then the shots sound and we realize with the terror that seized us at the madhouse that those that fall by the way are the litter that we leave. An adrenalin unnatural as lust in a dying flesh goads us into renewed, terminal haste, and my kit seems lighter and grows lighter still when Danny shouts, 'The stove! Throw it away!' and I unhook the all-but-forgotten blower-stove from where it is dangling and swaying from my kit and cast it aside.

At last the guards themselves tire and we slow down into our usual automaton's trudge, but now the adrenalin that powered us has petered out beyond even terror's reach, and my legs are floundering as though straw-stuffed or dropsical with stopped and pooling blood, and my ears are singing and my eyes are dry and hot and sometimes I sneeze, repeatedly and with an exuberance that is little short of obscene. As obscene is it when staff suddenly passes us, but, unaccountably, heading in the direction from which we came, and, although his face is as dour as ever, his flesh is glowing and trim and his gait openly contemptuous of our spi-

ritless crawl. 'Did you see that?' I whisper to Danny,
but he looks at me as though I am mad and when I, a
few steps on, see staff sitting to one side, his head resting on his arms folded on his knees and our guard level-
ling his gun at him, tears we are to remember streaming
from his eyes, I know that I am, indeed, a little mad
and try to not hear the shot that shortly afterwards
sends wings blundering through the leaves.

Later, the hulk is walking beside me, his face quite
healed, and he tries to take back his bag, but I fight him
off, shouting that he doesn't *need* it any more, and, pre-
dictably, he is then Douglas, a halo like a soup plate on
a head that has no face, and I say, 'OK! OK!' but wearily
as though I pander to a fractious child. And then there
are the faces that are not phantoms', that should wrench
me back into normalcy but only serve to scramble the
real and the unreal into a *fresh* unreality that, like all
illusion, has the hard stone of its genesis at its core.

The first we pass is that of Tony and he is really
not at all that bad, he lying there, flat on his back, his
pince-nez slipped down on his nose, his eyes closed and
only the almost bloodless hole in his skull betraying
that he has not fallen asleep in some sun known only to
him, and I make to break ranks and wish him well, but
Danny jerks me back with as anguished as angry a cry.
Camel, though, is something else. But for the old black
coat that always flapped around him like a raven's
wings – 'Hardly fit, that, for a camel!' I insanely grin –
I would not know him, his face so smashed that only
one eye still glares from the gelatinous mess and the
jaw with its teeth swung up so sharply and far that it

seems to belong to quite some other corpse, and, even as I stare, the teeth, which were not clenched, clack together as though responding to some last shred of the brain.

Does that, without my willing it, so penetrate my trance that I suddenly know – and know it with an unshakable certainty – that there are only so many paces still left in me, which I then studiedly take and stop.

'Tom! What *is* it?' Danny asks, dropping back, his eyes wildly anxious, probing mine.

'I'm finished. Let them shoot me. Here! Now!' Incredulously I listen to myself saying that, as incredulously know that I am *meaning* it, that this is none of my strutting on a stage. 'Is that all heroism is?' I detachedly wonder. 'One step the other side of despair?'

'Don't talk shit, man!' Danny yells. 'It's just nerves. I've been *watching* you getting weird.'

'Weird or not, that's the way it is.' Under any other circumstances the pompousness in my voice would have made me howl. 'My legs are *finished*! *Dead*! If you touch me, I'll fall down.'

'Oh, come *on*, mate! It can't be *that* bad!' and he tries to drag me by my arm and I immediately plummet to my knees, my feet not having moved from their stand, and our guard that cried is at once there, shouting, half-heartedly brandishing his gun, and I look at him and my eyes are telling him all that he needs to know and, slowly, he levels the gun.

'No!' Danny screams, knocking the barrel aside, seizing the guard by the shoulders, pleading with him with an abjectness that does not shame. 'Don't shoot him!

He's my friend. Help me get him on my back,' and he bends down in front of me and the guard hesitates for a second that seems as long as a life, then struggles me onto Danny's back, and Danny says, 'Hold tight,' and surges to his full height, but I'm begging to be put down, hysterically sobbing now that it is no use, and he shouts, 'Shut up, you cunt! You're all I have *left*! Hold tight, or I'll bash you again between the eyes!' and I hold tight, Danny gripping my thighs, his kit slung now to his front, my arms encircling his neck in the manner of a mother with a child, which image discomforts me with an acuteness that dismays.

I slip in and out of consciousness, the fever in me now rapidly taking hold, my bouts of sneezing becoming ever more frequent and prolonged, but the incidences of unconsciousness are very brief, my arms instinctively tightening round Danny's neck and jolting me back into sense each time the darkness looms. Sometimes those about us, shamed into a hankering for some finer self and vengefully proud that one of us, at least, is being spared when – according to the Krauts – he should be dead, offer to take turns carrying me, and Danny gruffly thanks them but says, no, he's fine, and they seem to respect him for that too, understanding perhaps – as do I – that his mate is his mate and is not to be bandied about any more than a wife. That makes me feel good in even the places that hunger has lamed, but as Danny, bandy-legged from the load he bears, grimly stomps on through the snow, only his history of running and weightlifting sustaining him now, and I hear his empty belly rumbling, as also the occasional fart as a foot comes down too hard, hear even his sinews and bones cracking as he adjusts his load, almost hear even the blood pumping through his veins, I begin to feel like a child in a womb and am back to the image of the mother and child and the discomfort that that image breeds.

Do I not pity him? Christ, am I a stone? Of course I pity him! What is more, I feel *pain* – a pain that is aggravated by the guilt of my knowing that I am causing *him* pain – which arguably could make my pain the fiercer of the two. But what can I do? Were I to struggle free of him and be shot, that would cause him an *ultimate* pain and reduce my dying to the petty and selfish act of a perverted will, particularly now that I find that my impulse towards death is waning with every step we take. So I go on riding him like some hideous succubus – an image, this, which I prefer to that of the child – and the trees click past in a slow computation of our going and the shots, and sometimes screams, continue to ring out above the funereal shuffle of our feet, and we begin to wonder with a renewal of immediate terror if the plan is to keep us moving till we have *all* fallen out and been shot and that was their goal all along.

But then, suddenly, the forest opens out onto a vast sweep of cold but clear sky, and the stars are so bright, so close – and so *unexpected* – that I involuntarily duck my head as before a still overhanging branch, and there is a grass underfoot that is largely free of snow and I can tell from the way Danny's body slants and his feet take a firmer purchase of the earth, that we are moving quite sharply downhill as into a valley, and the prisoners are

breaking up into groups and heading for various clus-
ters of lights seemingly haphazardly scattered over the
darkness below.

The guard that helped me onto Danny's back leads
about a hundred of us to one of the nearer groups of
lights and it turns out to be a farmhouse and cottage
with – judging by the sounds – a pigsty and chicken-
run and, above all, a barn piled high with straw where
the guard says we will sleep and the already bedded-
down cows regard us with the unflappability of beasts
used to sharing their universe with men. Danny lets me
slip then from his back into the straw, then straightens
up with a howl of anguish that at last turns the heads of
the cows and crashes down beside me even as I pass out
for that night's final time.

When I again wake, the cows are gone and pigeons
are fluttering and huffing on the roof-beams and traf-
ficking in and out of the open door. I am lying in a
swathe of sunlight as white and warming as a spread
sheet and a fine straw-dust is whirling and weaving in
the sun's long reaching through the barn. Outside,
there is an uproar of cluckings and grunts and the more
leisurely lowing of a cow, but there is no trace of a
human voice, as there is no trace of a startled farmer
querying our invasion of his farm. I am the only one
awake, the straw bristling with flung-wide, inanimate
legs and arms, and I become aware that my kit has been
slipped from my shoulders and is now pillowing my
head, an insistent hardness in the curve of my neck at
first puzzling me, then, at once as an apparition, declar-
ing itself to be my one of our two guns. At that, I turn

my head, sharply and afraid, the previous night back with me with the wholeness and clarity of a dream just dreamed, but his breathing beside me is even and deep and his face cleared of strain as a child's. Cautiously, I reach out and touch his cheek, his body again moving against mine in an act of fortitude beyond belief, but he does not stir and I trace his lips with a finger, possessing him, then sink back into sleep as into a coma, my hand still inarticulately outstretched.

Then he is straddling me, cuffing me under the chin, the shadows grown long, the cows, back from pasture and their milking, ambling through the door into the barn. 'Hey, you dead?' he shouts. 'I been hauling a corpse?' and he gets off me and I sit up and he says, 'Look what I've brought,' and he holds up six eggs and I stare at them, battling to comprehend.

'You been robbing the fowls?'

'Nah. Guard there,' and he gestures and I see our guard is kipping just a few feet from us and grinning like he's forgotten he's a Kraut, 'said we must go round to all the farms for food if we don't want to starve, so we all split up and knock, one at a time, at a door and, each time, a hand comes out and puts an egg in your hand like the missus in there is paying you to go away. So I eat one and save one and here's your share. But eat them *slowly*, mate, because this is rich stuff that the old gut's forgotten about and some of the blokes are knowing their mistake.'

'I must eat them *raw*? You know we don't have the stove any more.'

He laughs. 'Nah, man! They're already *boiled*. Salt

in the water too. Guard says they all know the war is as good as over, so the missus behind the hand is one frightened Frau that's not going to make you eat the eggs raw!'

So I throttle back my belly and nibble at the eggs like some twitchy-nosed mouse, and ask the guard what the fuck is going on and when do we march again, and he says there will be no more marching, that the chain of command is all but smashed, and then he looks at me and adds, his ingrown taciturnity of the peasant at last opening out into the full horror of what he knows, that we were to have been marched even further south into the mountains and then shot, but the route to there has now been cut.

'But can't they still massacre us *here*?' and a fresh terror is up and clawing at me at the thought.

'No. These are good people. They would not be permitting that.'

'So? Where *do* we go from here?'

'Be patient. Soon they will be coming to take you home.'

'And you?'

'I, too, will be going home. To my mother, who is alone. And,' and he pauses, looking at me with the desolateness of the condemned, 'a priest. I need absolution – for these,' and he holds out his working man's hands, then turns his back to me and, later, pretends to be asleep, and I finish off the eggs, my stomach absorbing them with the sensuousness of a snail a leaf, and it is only then that I remember what my mother always told me about eggs.

'Hey,' I say to Danny, 'you know that eggs can stop you shitting for a week?'

'Who the fuck cares?' he grins and, as if on cue, two hands – like the hands that held the eggs – are setting down two buckets of milk just outside the door, and we whoop and apportion it, each of the hundred mouths getting little more than a few sips but savouring them all the same, and I realize that I am not sneezing any more and that the hot dry eyes are moist with what, shamingly, just might be tears.

In the morning, we try out my legs and, at first, I am walking as if they are two sticks, but, later, they loosen up and I take my place in the egg-scrounge, which means that, in the case of Danny and myself, the harvest is doubled and we land up with more eggs than we can comfortably – or wisely – consume in one day. So we hold half over till the following day and I suggest to Danny that we take that day off, but he says, 'No way! We must grab what we can. *Now*! Jesus, they can't go *on* giving us eggs! It would take a million hens for that!' And that very next day he is proved right, but very pleasingly so, the eggs beginning to be replaced by a duo of sometimes a slice of wurst and sometimes a slice of black, home-baked bread. 'This is the life!' he exults. 'Goodies from heaven, like the Bible says! Or are we back at the start and I am a he and you – what are you, mate?' and he makes a pass at my crotch which I slap aside, and I marvel at the difference that a few eggs and a sip of milk can make, although the difference is mainly in the mind and the body still so sad an also-ran.

The valley round us plays its part in our rejuvenation, it being now clearly spring – the snow only holding out in the more sheltered places and along the banks of the several streams – and the grass, green as a baize and even as though scythed, is as spangled with flowers as a young girl's dress spread for a picnic or a love, and, once, Danny grips my arm and says, 'Look!' and there it stands – a stag – massive antlers flaring, nose snuffing the wind, and the whole as out of place – and beautiful – as some mythical beast magically raised.

We pass through a village once – that is if it can be called that, it consisting of not much more than a post office and an inn – but the inn is alive with light and talk and the beery smell attracts Danny like a lamppost a dog. 'A pub!' he exclaims. 'Let's go in!' and I say he's crazy, that they will throw us out on our arse, and he says that they have already done much worse to us than that, and we go in.

The silence is only momentary as we come through the door, but still long enough to assure us that we have been seen. Then there is a concerted and studied effort to convince us that we are no longer seen, and we sit down at a table in a corner, our knees touching under its minuscule round, and look up to find that the proprietor, ensconced behind his stubby bar, is not at all averse to our knowing that he is seeing us, is, in fact, studying us with an intentness that is as speculative as it is unashamed. Then, nodding to himself as though arriving at a decision, he heaves himself out from behind the bar and heads for us across the hardly bigger than a bedroom's floor, his paunch flopping like a half-filled sack, his eyes steely in a face that is otherwise all cherry-red cheeks and snow-white fuzz fit for a Santa Claus.

'You are English?' he says, rather than asks, one gnarled hand resting on the table with a heaviness that makes me wince, and Danny says, 'Yes,' unabashed, and I, nervy as all hell, nod though I'm not. 'Wait here,' and the hand that was on the table is swinging back to the bar, and I look at Danny and he looks at me and I say, 'This is it. Let's duck,' but he laughs, 'Don't fuss, mate! You're forgetting. We won the war, we call the shots,' and I say, 'OK, *you* tell him that when he gets back,' and then the old guy *is* coming back, but now holding a tray from which he unloads two tankards of draught beer, two small glasses of schnapps and a plate of liverwurst, thickly sliced.

I stare at him, bemused, Danny now hardly less taken aback. 'Please,' I say in my best Kraut, 'there must be some mistake. We have no money to pay for this.'

'I am not asking for money,' he retorts, his English excellent, a smile transforming him. 'Now eat, drink,' and, to me, 'Money is not feminine,' and goes.

We look at the food, the drink, the schmaltz on the walls, listen to the schmaltz spewing from the bar's ancient radio, and I pick up one of the glasses of schnapps and say, showing off, 'You are supposed to drink this first,' and Danny picks up the other glass and we chink them and he says, 'Our first night out,' and I crack back, 'I thought you were never going to ask,' and he kicks me in the shins as we hit back the schnapps with a gasp, and someone at last glances round and slyly grins. Then we steadily eat our way through the wurst, down the beer, and, when we leave, the radio is belting out that sloppy song about the bint that is forever standing under a lamppost beside a barrack's gate, and, outside, we, too, bellow out the words till long after the music can no longer be heard, and hook an arm around each other's neck, we staggering, then, over a radiant, grown turbulent earth.

Almost I begin to insanely accept that Danny was right – that this *is* the sweetest Eden of them all – but, the next day, we are standing outside the barn before the start of the scrounge-around and the guard grabs my arm and whispers, 'Look!' jerking his head towards where the forest ends, and there is no mistaking them – the black caps, black boots, black gloves – the whole that of stick-figures dipped in the blackness of a drying blood, of toys fashioned by a malevolent hand, but the menace still there and, incredibly, something of the tawdry sadness, the dusty standing on an abandoned stage, of the woman in the song.

'We in danger?' I whisper back, the old terror immediately aroused.

'No, it is too near the end now. Also, it is not the first time I am seeing them there.' Then drily, 'Maybe they are wishing they were me.'

So it is not they that are the threat. But omens, they fade back into the forest, though not so readily back into my mind.

It is four days later when they arrive. Danny and I are dawdling back from a scrounge, the sun low in the west, when we see them coming down the slope to the barn, disappearing behind its blind side, maybe ten of them, walking single file like guinea fowl back home. When we get to the barn, they have already hassled the guys out — the guard, too, he standing to one side, shivering like snow's on the ground again and he with nothing on.

Their whatever he is — he is not flashing any rank — swanks over to us, hardware truculently in his hands. 'You prisoners?' he asks, voice high and thin like they've hacked off his balls, squat nose flaring like a bull scenting cow. We nod and he snaps, 'Get over there,' gesturing with the gun to where the other guys are standing, bowed legs for a runt already wheeling him round.

'Who says?' Danny growls, giving him the eye, and he whirls back, moistly petulant mouth tightening into a snarl, startlingly white eyelashes exclamatory as a girl's. 'The US of A, soldier!' he shrills, the bowed legs trying to straighten into a tighter squeezing of their oval of air, and now all of us get to laughing till we're feeling we'll fall down, as much of hysteria in our laughter as the black baying of our rage, and he waits, entrapped and knowing it, and we stop and he says, sulkily, letting us stand where we are, 'OK. Show's over. This guy' — gun's barrel levelled now at the guard — 'What do you want us to do? Shoot him and let him lay, or kick him in the ass and let him go?'

Ashamedly, we face the guard, ashamed that we should have been asked to be his judge, ashamed that any man should so tremblingly try to hide his fear while the eyes so mercilessly betray the last tatters of his pride. 'Remember,' the eyes implore of me, fawning as any about-to-beaten dog's, and I do — death again but a vagary of his will away, the night, with its shots and screams, the sudden antechamber of my own oblivion beyond recall.

Danny beats me to it, though, 'Neither,' he says, his tone thrusting at the runt like a blade. 'We don't shoot him and we don't kick him in the arse or anywhere else when we let him go. Right?' and he glances round at the rest of us and we say, 'Right!' as one, and the runt looks at us as though we are no better than the guard, then shouts, 'Vamoose!' flapping his gun as though he is shooing a fowl, and the guard stares at him, not understanding the word, and I, at last, say, 'Go, friend,' and our eyes meet over the barriers of blood and tribe for a moment that is endlessly prolonged. Then he flees, shamblingly, not even taking up what is his.

The shot rings out as he is about to round the barn and slams him against its wall, but he does not fall. Then there is a second shot and he begins to slide, one hand fumbling for a purchase on the wall, and I am running, and Danny is running, and we reach him as he hits the ground and rolls over, face to the sky. Blood is already pooling under him and spilling from his mouth, and I kneel beside him and take one of the peasant hands with its broken nails into mine, and he grips it with a frenzied strength and struggles to speak, the words bubbling up through the blood, as Danny raises, then cradles, his head. 'What is he saying?' Danny asks, his voice stolid with the helplessness of having watched many die. 'Something about his mother,' I say, striving for a similar submissiveness in the presence of death, and lean closer to the tortured mouth to hear, but the bubbling stops and, even as I watch, the desperate eyes still into their final, alienating glass.

Gently, Danny lays the head down and we pace, together, to where the rest are standing, rooted as though the bullets had struck them all. 'Why did you do it?' I ask of the runt, my voice oddly everyday's, the actor in me, even now, sincerely prompting that this is the way it should be done.

'For practice,' he says, his eyes insolently alive, and he casts around for his men's dutiful titter, but they are stonily silent, looking only at the ground, and, for the first time, something of an uneasiness seizes him and he turns back to us and begins to make like he doesn't understand, 'So why all the fuss? He was only a cocksucking Kraut. *All* Krauts suck cocks. Didn't you know that? Jesus, after all this time in camp, surely you are not *that* fucking dumb!'

'That cocksucker saved my life,' I say, still levelly. 'It's *you* that's a cocksucker, you goddam Yankee shit!'

His eyes tell me that I have gone too far as he has gone too far, but *he* is thinking that he sees a way out. 'Well, now,' he says, stretching it slow and long, again looking round at his men, 'why would a Kraut want to do that? What did you do for him that he would want to do that? Maybe here it's the other way around. Maybe here it's *you* that's the one. Yeah! You been sucking his cock, siphoning it when he's got the hots?'

Again I am too slow, as *he* is too slow. His head is still swinging round from its circling of his men, when Danny has tripped him onto his back, seized the rifle by the barrel, smashed its butt into the again rising face

– smashed the face again and again till teeth are spilling from it like corn from a cob, and the jaw is crushed, and the cheekbones, and it is beginning to look like another Camel down there on another sure spot for a spook. But then the runt's men at last move in, wrench the rifle from Danny's hands, wrench him away from the blinded, heaving mess on the ground, let him go again when his own blindness heals and he sits down and stares at the nothing between his knees. Then they pick up the runt and cart him off like he's meat, and one looks back and yells, 'Never saw a thing!'

For the first time since we came, we knock on the farmhouse door and the farmer, a gnarled root of a man with eyes clear as the nearby streams, nods with no hatred in him and says, to me – did the dead man tell him I understand German and why is it no longer so easy for me to say 'Kraut' or 'guard'? – that he saw it all and here is a blanket, and he goes with us and we roll the body onto the blanket, and he hoses away the blood and receives the blanket into his home with careful and slow hands, closing the door and saying that they will trace the mother and everything will be arranged.

Then we wait for them to fetch us, not knowing which way to go, not any longer really *wanting* to go, our roots – incorrigible parasites that they have become – already seeking anchorage in a transience of spring, its no longer snow-fed streams' ebbing flow, a wandering stag that fortuitously stood, an inn with a radio that sang of a ghost of the mind, a dead body behind a locked door that will not open to us again. Mercifully, the waiting is not long. Even as dusk comes, they are here – four trucks with another batch of Yanks who barely give us time to grab our kits, give us no time at all for looking back, thunder us for two hours through a landscape we will never see.

The airfield is not what it used to be. The signs – one tellingly askew – still speak of 'Flugplatz', but it is Yanks and poms that are rushing round, loud-hailers in their hands, and the runways bounce the planes, the craters still but rawly filled, and the terminal's window, smashed, haggardly gapes like that mouth I am struggling to not recall. The trucks offload us alongside the runway nearest the terminal and a pommy staff, well over the hill, droopy moustache as mournful as his hangdog eyes, comes to us with a clipboard and sorts out our nationalities, units, names. 'Sleep here tonight,' he drones. 'Right here. Nice night, so there's no problem there. Tomorrow, sparrowfart, all onto the planes. Brits on planes to Blighty and straight to your homes. Rest' – what, I suddenly wonder, happened to the *Russian*? – dead in a forest, bones stripped clean, or did he again swap camps before the axe fell? – 'rest on separate planes to Blighty and into camps and wait there till your own chaps take you home.'

Suddenly it is here again, crashing down between us like a sawn-through tree – the separation that had faced us once before, but had been thwarted by a vagary of war. Had we, like children living only for today, really thought that there would be no second reckoning, that, then, the tree would *still* not fall? I look at him and he looks back, our eyes the eyes of creatures that, spines crushed, reach out to each other across a widening gulf, and I raise my hand. 'How long,' I ask, my voice struggling to be my age, 'will we be in those camps?'

'You a South African?' I nod. 'One month, three months, who can say?' Then – sensing my pain? – '"Camps" doesn't mean *prison* camps! You will be able to get around, get to know Blighty while you can.' At once, we are what we were, our months expanding into years, our todays our blind sole unit for the measuring of time, and when, leaving, he indicates a monolith of food parcels beside the runway and, with a first glimmering of humour, adds, 'All yours,' we cry out as at our murder or rape and rush to cart parcels away to where each of us has decided to sleep, and are then no longer a hundred funny men in yesterday's funny clothes, but a hundred desperately sick and messily amoral deviates and servitors of greed making whoopee under as sick and gibbous a moon.

Leaning against our twenty parcels each, knowing well that we can never take them with us, but, as in the case of our pending parting of the ways, not admitting it – vowing, rather, to defend to the last man out of two this so useless a hoard – we slowly eat our way through a parcel from our stock and take the measure of each other with the ancient serpent-eyes of the replete. 'Hey,' Danny says, solemnly as though I would not be knowing this, 'we are free,' and again we size each other up, but now there is more than our being free to our sniffing of each other's sides, and we have been achingly aware of this ever since the turmoil at the barn. There is an explosiveness in us as in a cat's fur before a storm, a primal, reactive energy that bloodshed and death breed, that seeks now to out as every cumulative force must, whether it be a lava or merely a pus, and I shift uncomfortably as one holding back an embarrassing wind.

'I say we are free!' Danny now yells. 'Free to do as we fucking well want! So wrestle, you!' and he's all over me like the big kid he sometimes was at camp, teeth nuzzling into my neck, making as if to sever its veins, throat roaring like a ravening wolf's, lissome, cunning body twisting round me like it has no bones, one pinioning switching to another with unpredictable shufflings of technique, but never any grabbing of the balls, breaking of the skin, drawing of blood. We laugh and pant, roll around like angry cats, though we are never that, lie for long moments, rigidly entwined, eyes staring into eyes, breath meshing into breath, then start again, knocking over our parcels' stack, not caring about that, not letting the tumbling parcels interrupt the intricate subterfuges of our limbs.

Then, suddenly, I want out, am inwardly crying for him to stop, not even thinking, though, to cry out aloud, for that would be to expose my state. Is he feeling the same? Why do we both no longer laugh or shout, mutter picturesque and meaningless threats? Does he, too, realize that this is no longer a childish game, that, stealthily, it has become the oldest game of all? Silently we wrestle on, seriously now as though we sought a death, eyes unseeing, fixed, as eyes painted on a mask – or those that watch a sky beyond a sky, a self within a self? Convulsed, he stops first, face to my face, permitting that I overpower him, knowing that I cannot, then flings himself off me, lies, face down, alone.

In the morning, dawn not yet showing in the east, he is up and at a nearby tap, and I see that he is wiping the stain off the front of his pants with a wet palm. When he is finished, I get up and ostentatiously do the same, but he does not react, just stands there, moodily staring at the busyness of the planes. So I say to him, straight, carefully censoring any pleading out of my voice, 'You still wanting me to visit you because, if so, how must I get to a place when I don't even know where the fuck it is?' He does not answer me, just takes one of his mother's letters out of his kit and tears off the portion of it that carries his home address, then passes that to me and goes on staring at the planes. 'Well, puh-lease,' I say, sneering louder than any clown, 'don't do me any favours if it's going to bust your gut!' But then I notice that his hands are trembling and that his moodiness is something quite else, so I turn him round to face me, which he quite willingly does, and now I do plead, almost hearing time running out, 'Look we wrestled and we were randy, so we came. That is *all*. I didn't bugger you and you didn't bugger me like so many of the guys in the camps were doing all the time. We were free and we were happy fit to bust. So we bust and now you're wanting me to slash my wrists? For *that*? Get lost!'

It is a good try, but, deep down, a niggling doubt as to the *truth* of it is fluttering like a raven trapped in a well, and the staff is coming with his clipboard and shouting, 'Brits form up!' and Danny is hurrying to obey, his hand hardly having touched mine, the lights going out one by one as I watch the distance between us lengthening, when he suddenly turns round, yells, 'You don't visit me, I'll bash you! You hear?'

'Up you!' I yell back and I'm not sure, but I think he grins.

From the beginning, it is as though some exotic flower has been uprooted from its habitat and transplanted to an alien climate and soil. Without Danny, I am like a man from whom an essential part has been hacked, but, as the days, then weeks, pass, it becomes clear that an almost ritual nostalgia is deadening the first, intolerable pain. Why 'days and weeks'? Why don't I just up and *go* to that small village with the slip of paper with his address on it inquiringly in my hand? The answer is as simple as it is frustrating and sad: there is just no way that I *can*.

The 'camp' of which the staff spoke is not that in the usual sense of the word, but a street of vacated cottages in a seaside town where the sea is more often grey than blue, the rain coming down without warning and frequently, though it is supposed to be spring. It *is* true that I can go where I want, provided that I report to the repatriation office each morning to find out if I have not perhaps been allocated a seat on a plane. Then there are the sessions with a psychiatrist and dietician who mostly tell me what I already know, namely, that I am a little crazy and I must take up to an hour to eat a plate of food because my stomach is as shrunken as a punctured balloon.

So I take to walking beside the sea on the bright days, envying the gregarious gulls, but inwardly emulating their contradictorily solitary cries, and sometimes I sit on the edge of the nearby downs, watching the white woolly sheep latch onto as woolly a green sward. I also take the train to London now and then, it being but a whisker away, and pay the mandatory visits to the Tower and Tussaud's, but spend most of my daily stipend from the repatriation office on tickets for plays which *do* take me out of myself to the degree that I need.

Once I even accept the invitation of a whore who could have been my mother, but only manage to get it fully up when it is already in. 'You been a prisoner of war?' she asks, not unkindly, when I have paid her and am buttoning up my pants, and I nod and she adds, 'Cunt is still too rich for you, lad. Get your boyfriend out of your system and try me again,' and I don't even expostulate at that, just slink out of there with my sullenly slack tail literally between my legs.

Then I have been there a month and I go into the office to check on the planes and the guy there, who knows me by now, asks, 'Would there be some who are calling you just plain "Tom Smith" instead of these fancy names I'm looking at here?' I say, 'Could be,' and stiffen up, somehow sensing what's coming next. 'Would this be for you?' and he hands me one of those message slips that these red tape types leave next to their phones, and I can see it is dated the day before and it reads, 'From Danny to Tom Smith – where are you, mate? Is one kick in the arse not enough?'

'It is for me,' I say, trying for calm.

'And you understand what he's saying there?' and I

see that this guy is looking at me like I'm bad news that will liven up his day.

'I understand. What I don't understand is how he managed to get through to me *here*.'

'No problem. If he knows you are waiting to be repatriated, he'll know where to look in the book for a number that'll put him through. You want to answer him?' and I see there are figures on the slip which I had thought were just bureaucratic crap. 'You can use this phone if you want.'

'No hurry,' I say, and fold the slip and put it in a pocket, and get out of there, deeply troubled that I didn't accept the offer of the phone and wondering why. Back in the room that I share with three other guys, but they are all out now on this dead town, I work it out that I am *afraid*, that it is as if Danny has gone in behind a closed door to change his gear and, if I open the door, he will be standing there looking like nobody I know, and I stripped, then, of a dream that I cannot afford to lose, that I want should *stay* a dream. Linked to that is a growing longing to be back under a sky where the sun wheels forever before going down, to walk through a wideness whose very bleakness is purity of a kind, to be freed from this incestuous, pretty island that makes me stoop as though I'm walking in under a never high enough door.

Four days later, the Repat guy says, 'Come again. Round about five. I may have something for you.' So I have an uneasy lunch, my appetite – for once – well below par, try to sleep, to read, most of the time nibble at my nails, then, at five, call again and he says,

'Tomorrow night, ten p.m., a seat for you,' and I yell and wring his hand, then go out and at once – my separation from him now certain – a renewed longing to see Danny, to convert what was becoming a myth back into a reality of flesh and breath, overwhelms me, and I know that I *can* still do it – *will* still do it – and almost run back to the room for money for a ticket and to exchange my usual shirt and slacks for something fancier, cursing myself and flinging things about with the abandon of one whom the devil drives.

The sun is setting by the time I make it to the station and buy a ticket to the little village where Danny lives. There are few passengers on the platform at this late hour on a weekday and a timetable on a hoarding tells me that it is fifty minutes yet before the train leaves, so I stride up and down the platform, willing the minutes to pass, then suddenly realize that Danny does not even know I am coming and head for a telephone box, rummaging in my pockets for the expat's message slip with Danny's phone number on it, but, of course, it is not there, but in the slacks I have just taken off and flung across the bed, and no time left now still to go back to the room. 'Jesus!' I think, panic stirring in me, 'What if he's *not there*? Gone to a pub, perhaps, to whoop it up with all his other pals?' and something cruelly like jealousy thrusts through me at the latter half of that thought, but it does not put a damper on my desire to be there – does, in fact, *fuel* that desire till I unthinkingly grab at its terminal spasm in my crotch.

When the train draws out, it is already full night, which means I will not be seeing anything of the intervening countryside as I will not be seeing anything of it coming back, which thought oddly depresses me, facing me, as it does, with this strange, blind hiatus in my life. My reflection in the window stares back at me like an ectoplasmic second self the glass has snared, and I eventually jerk down the sash, that relentless scrutiny unnerving me more than I care to admit, but the looming night, with its interruptively meaningless lights, is little better than my looming face, and the alternating of darkness and light so mesmerizes me that I nearly don't see the signboard as it hurtles past and the train crashes to a halt.

Only I get off, onto cinders – the train having overshot the platform through, conceivably, not expecting anyone to alight at such an hour in such a place – which, in my case, is as well because, just across the line from me, is a signpost pointing the way to 'High Street', which is the street I want and I am thus saved the trouble of having to make inquiries at the 'station' that consists of little more than a sheltered bench and a ticket office no bigger than a booth.

'High Street' seems as little deserving of its status as the station, it clearly being the only street and more a rural lane than a street, frogs sounding in a distant pond or stream, a cricket screeching like a rusty hinge nearer at hand and the clean, green smell of meadows, spiced with a faint pepperiness of cowpats, crowding in on me like memories of an innocence that – as in the case of Danny? – died at the first thrust that so oddly no longer thrusts in the screaming of my dreams. As once before, I ask myself *why* is it that I have not dreamt of that since the day in the sun when Danny said I cried in my sleep, and stop, bemused – by what? – a coming to terms? – a hastening to a consummation that, through its subsuming all else, will finally heal?

A dark excitement possesses me and I hurry on past the first signs of a communal life – a post office, a tearoom, a shop, all three closed, then a pub bright with light, murmurous with the muted revelry of respectable men – and pause, then, to glance at my watch and am amazed that my entire journeying up to here has taken up less than half an hour of my time. All these weeks, Danny only half an hour away and only now do I come? Ashamed – too late – I start checking on the cottages set well back from the road, know the one that is Danny's even before I see the number on its gate, it being as beat-up as he had always described it to me, the garden as interestingly unkempt as the growing-tatty thatch, a shed to one side minus most of its panes. Warily, feeling like a wraith strayed back into a world where it no longer belongs, I pace up the cracking paving of the path, lift, let fall, the knocker on the door.

By the bossiness of her stance, the challenging sharpness of her 'Yes?' I know that she must be Danny's mum, but, otherwise, she is not at all what I expect. What *did* I expect? A little old lady with withered but still rosy cheeks, iron-grey hair tied in a bun, dumpy body redolent of lavender and bread-dough, faded blue eyes about to break into a smile? Instead, she is thin as a string, face smooth and old ivory as a china doll's, tinted-blue hair tightly permed, black eyes snapping as they rake me from head to toe, no sign of the fragrances my mind supposed.

She *is* little, though, so much so that her head tilts as she looks up at me and again asks, 'Yes?' her voice a perceptible shade higher than before.

I find my tongue then. 'Good evening. Could I see Danny please?'

'You're not from here,' she counters, flatly, as though that would be reason enough for her to slam the door.

'No, but I was in the prisoner of war camps with your son.'

'How do you know he's my son?'

'You look like the way he described you to me. He spoke of you all the time,' I lie, laying it on.

'Oh.' Then, 'Well, come in then,' and she lets me into a very large, all-purpose room, comfortably but shabbily furnished in no particular style, two doors, closed, opening off it and a steep, abrupt stair – more a ladder than a stair – leading up to a landing with two more doors, which surprises me because the cottage, when I viewed it from the gate, and even from closer up, had not seemed to me to be all that high.

'Danny! Someone to see you!' she calls from the foot of the stair, her voice unfaltering and strong, and we stand around in an uncomfortable awareness of each other till one of the doors slams open and he is hastening down the stair, tightening the cord of an old but oddly opulent dressing-gown that makes him look as if I'm meeting up with the wrong guy and sets me to thinking that, it being the hot and clear night that it is, he is not wearing anything underneath, that being his way.

'Tom!' he exclaims, his face briefly lit by the delight in his voice, then again carefully controlled, and I expect him to embrace me, but his eyes flick aside to his mother and he merely shakes my hand, though holding it in both of his, and says to his mother, his voice now as studiedly on an even keel as his face, 'Mum, this is Tom Smith. The one I am always telling you about.'

'Oh, *that* one,' she says as though the cat I have not seen has brought me in, and she does not extend her hand or smile.

'Yes, *that* one,' he clearly mocks, then looks at his watch. 'Time still to celebrate at the pub. Wait here till I get some duds on my skin,' and I watch him going up the stair, the step of his slippered feet – *slippers?* – *him?* – as nimble as when I first met him, the muscles of his calves moving with a fluid clarity and grace.

'I nearly didn't know him in the dressing-gown,' I try to joke as we wait. 'It's a far cry from the camps!'

'It was his father's. He's very fond of it. And, yes, it *is* a far cry from the camps, Mr Smith. So much so that I hope you have not come to remind him of them, I being the one that has to cope with what is still a very sick boy. He has, I suppose, told you about his wife?' and she says 'suppose' as though we are two snotty kids who have been telling each other dirty stories behind her back.

'Yes, he has. And about his father too, if it comes to that,' and I feel smug at my tone's implying that there's a lot more to be said about *him* than about the wife.

She seems to catch it because she snaps right back,

'Well, there's nothing to say about his father except that he's dead. It's what his *wife* has done to him that's killing him now. God knows I have done my best to get him interested in some other girl – one in particular – but he just sits around, here or in the pub, and, to be quite frank, Mr Smith,' and she looks at me with an emotion so akin to hatred that a chill hits my spine, 'I have the feeling that your visit is going to be the worst thing to happen to him since the war.'

Then he's coming back, still uncharacteristically dressed in stylish slacks, a not inexpensive open-neck shirt and slip-on, low-heeled shoes that make me feel like a soldier in hobnail boots all over again.

'By the way,' he asks, as he comes off the bottom step, 'why didn't you phone before you came? Didn't the repat office give you my message with the phone number and all?'

'No,' I say, looking surprised as I lie without shame, instinctively knowing where telling the truth will lead. 'Not a word from anyone there.'

'Bastards,' he says, but without rage. 'And your gear? You didn't bring any gear?'

'It's only half an hour to here,' I now desperately evade, beginning to feel boxed-in, the incompleteness of what I am saying hanging out like a rebellious shirt-tail, but he does not seem to see anything wrong.

'Tom can sleep with me,' he says, turning to his mother. 'I'll lend him what he needs.'

'Don't talk nonsense, Danny! Yours is only a three-quarter bed and you're two grown men. You can't both sleep on *that*!'

'In camp, we both slept on one *bunk* not much bigger than that.'

'Well, you're not doing that here! You can lend Mr
Smith a pair of your pyjamas, but he's sleeping down
here in the spare room.'

'Let's go,' he says, his mouth tightening, his hand
gripping my arm.

'And don't stay out all night and don't come back
drunk,' she nags at his back as we reach the door, and
he looses my arm and strides back to her, and she
draws back a pace when she sees his eyes.

'Listen!' he hisses, his hands on her shoulders, his
face thrusting so close to hers that she jerks her head
aside. 'I have had enough of you telling me what to do!
This *Mr Smith*, as you keep calling him, is my *mate* and
we are going to stay out as long as we feel like it, and
we are going to go on boozing till the piss runs down
our legs if we want it that way. Understand?' and she
begins to weep, and he leaves her and we go out, he,
strangely, not slamming the door.

'Sorry about that,' he says, his fists moodily rammed
into the pockets of his slacks as we march – unconsciously in step – down the road. 'She's changed. Like
you and I have changed,' and he pauses for a long moment in which I sense that a nothing that is everything
is continuing to be said. 'She was never like this before
I went away. Always fitted in with my moods, would
advise me if I needed it, but not doing that if she saw I
wanted to work something out by myself, and, what
was the *greatest*, growing old *nicely*, like every bloke
wants that his mum should. But now? Well, you've seen

her – do this, don't do that, shove it up this or that
bint's cunt, even though I am not even thinking that
way right now, and, shittiest of all, treating any bloke
that visits me the way she did *you* tonight and doing
herself over like she wants to be a girl again instead of
my mum.' We walk in silence a while, then he sighs and
shakes his head with a hopelessness that is not him at
all, 'I would leave her – she's got her pension and all –
but the trouble is I *understand* her. She nearly lost me
with the war, so now she knows how *that* feels and
she's doing all she can to not have to face it again.
Christ alone knows how it will all end.'

Then we turn into the pub with its willing spigots,
gleaming tankards, as gleaming copperware on the
walls, and, oblivious to all else about us, drink quietly
and slowly but *thoroughly*, as men do when besieged by
intimations of deprivation and pain. At one stage, he
asks me how long I am staying and I dart away from
that like a shot-at bird, saying, 'Let's not worry about
that now,' and go to fetch us another two beers, and we
return to our clothing of dead men, spent events, in the
ephemeral skins of our words, but not being honest
about it, sneaking round Douglas' name as though it is
a black hole and he has never been.

Then the publican warns of a closing and still we
have not achieved what we *really* set out to do, which
was to again see, to *know*, each other as we were *then* –
to see and know despite the distorting glass between us
of the now's new ambiences, changed circumstances,
grown alien strictures and codes. The beer, however,
has seduced us into a bleary joyousness that we know is

fake even as we spread our legs for it, and we leave the pub as once we left an inn in another place and time, singing the same song as then, singing it all the way down the road, arms encircling necks, till we stop at the right gate and copiously piss, song winding down in us like a nickelodeon running out of coins.

The door is locked, but Danny has his own key and we go in to a single light's burning in the communal room, but there is no sign of Danny's mother and he points upstairs and pulls a face, then checks on the room where I'm supposed to sleep and grunts that she has 'fixed' it and do I want to eat, and I say, no, I have had enough chips and pasties at the pub. Then he says he knows I don't want any fucking pyjamas, it being this hot, and I say of course I don't, and he looks at me, teetering a little from the booze, and says, very gently, possessively, 'My mate,' then adds, turning round at the door as he leaves, 'I am *sorry*. But I've hurt her enough for one night,' and I lie awake for a long time, not because I don't understand what he said, but because I understand it unsettlingly too well.

When I wake, the sun, warmly and rousingly in the room, is exposing the latter's uncompromising barrenness – the narrow iron cot, ancient wardrobe that tilts a little when I touch it, cracked china jug and basin on a stand, and, in one corner, a laundry basket and a miscellany of mops and brooms. There is water in the jug and I pour some into the basin and slosh it on my face and comb my wet fingers through my hair. The night's drunken expansiveness has shrivelled into a small but persistent knot of pain behind my eyes and I stand, listening for sound and drying my face and hands on my still clean handkerchief because I am not finding any towel, but the cottage seems as silent as though all but I have abandoned it in an hour of its need. Then I take hold of the doorknob, at long last polished, and at once remember that, sometime in the night, it had turned, but I had not responded because I had not known whether it was Danny wanting in or she checking to see who was sleeping where.

Then I go out, closing the door, and Danny – presumably hearing that – shouts, 'In here, Tom!' and I go through the other of the two doors opening out of the central room, and it is the kitchen and Danny is sitting at a plain wooden table and spooning up milk and cereal with a lightly trembling hand. 'Belly up, mate,' he says, hooking a chair out from under the table with his foot and indicating the box of cereal and a glass jug of milk, and I see that his eyes are narrowed as a Chink's with a shared pain and his face is drawn.

I also then see that *she* is there, stirring something in a pot on the old-fashioned iron stove, her back turned, and I wish her a good morning, though my heart is not in it, and she says, 'Good morning, Mr Smith,' and Danny at once flings down his spoon, scattering cereal and milk like a bad child, and yells, 'Call him Tom, goddammit! It won't burn your tongue!' but she takes no notice, just goes on stirring whatever-it-is and finding other things for her hands to do, and Danny sits moodily watching me eat cereal that's tasting like straw, the ice between him and her thickening fit to skate on and he drumming with his spoon on the

table till it is getting as much on my nerves as hers
and I am wishing that I was anywhere but here.

Then I am finished and wanting to piss, but not
wanting to ask where's the toilet in this special brand
of a hell for two, and he says, 'Come, let me show you
around,' and we go out into the blessedly impersonal
sun and I piss behind the nearest hedge and he watches
me with sorrowing eyes, saying, 'Shit!' explosively, as
though he is spewing out a last gobbet of rage. There is
a fence with a stile at the back of the cottage and we
cross over into the field that he was always telling me
about in the camps, and although – like everything else
here – it is smaller than I had pictured it, it is as post-
card-pretty as he had described it, the grass seeding and
lush and the flowers, with their obligatory bees, all the
more having a ball for not being planned, and I say to
Danny that I can understand why dogs always want to
lie down in a place like this for a wriggle and a roll.

He grins, then – the first sign of a lightening of his
mood – and shows me the stream running along the
further boundary of the field, and we take off our socks
and shoes and wade in the brilliant shallow water,
going with its flow till its thin singing over the stones
passes into the wide quietness of a pool. Here the water
is deep and green as from a long bleeding of leaves, and
patches of lily pads are floating on it like giants' severed
ears, and there is a dankness all about as of florists or
crypts, and I am glad when we get to the gently noisy
weir a hundred yards on and the pool again becomes a
stream. Danny seems unfazed by the sombreness of the
pool – says, in fact, that this is where he always swims,

and leads me into some bushes a pace away, and we break out into a tiny glade of cropped-short grass which, he says, is his suntrap like we had at the one camp and maybe this is where we can again be what we once were, and still I do not tell him that time is running out on us more finally than any hurrying stream.

'Let's swim,' he says, dropping his socks and shoes, looking at me with challenging eyes.

'Here? Now? What *in*?' and I'm knowing my questions are making me sound like a question-machine.

'Your *skin*. What else? You gone all shy on me, mate?' and already he has shucked off shirt and slacks, is wriggling out of the jockstrap that shows he is still a jogging man.

'What if somebody comes?'

'We'll *see* them come. From *way* off, we'll see them come. And, anyway, the water's too cold for more than a quick in-and-out to get the booze out of our brains. So, come *on*! You're already the bum, standing there!' and he breaks back through the bushes and I hear him splash into the pool.

Hesitantly, I undress, get to stand on the weir, the overflowing, again clear water curling round my toes, and he mocks me as he thrashes around amongst the lily pads, and I dive in, and it's like smashing, head on, into cold iron, and I'm out again with a yell, but he has me by a leg, dragging me back, and is ducking me till I fight free and am again on the weir, then on the bank, shivering and feeling blue as a kingfisher on a reed, but my mind shining and clear as a just-polished lens.

Then he, too, is out and we are back in the clearing
and everything is coming together again as he drops
onto the grass and starts to roll around in it, making
like a dog, penis flailing out of the glistening bush of
the pubic hair and his eyes, shrewd as a satyr's, black as
a seal's, enticing me to join him in the perilous innocence of his world. But time is still running out for us
and I stand, vacuously grinning and sad, and he gets up
and puts his hands on my shoulders, his eyes asking
why and his body moving to cover mine though it is
still an arm's length away, and we turn and lie down on
the grass, side touching side, our eyes closed against the
sun.

'There's something you're not saying to me,' he
says, his voice resigned as though he already senses
what it is, and I tell him, then, my misery unfeigned –
but a certain cunning in me emphasizing that it could
not have happened otherwise – and he nods, his face
folding in upon itself, and we are silent again, listening
to the heedless joyousness of the birds – or is joy as for-
eign to them as pain? – and once two women pass a
few paces from us, chattering of their trivial affairs.

At last, he turns onto his stomach, looks down at
me, 'You will be back?' and I nod, compelled, his closeness – of breath, being, flesh – overwhelming me, the
strong, long line of his spine, buttocks, calves, reminding me of their carrying me out of death into life.

'Yes,' I whisper, 'I'll be back. As soon as they have
demobbed me, I'll be back.'

'Yes,' he, too, then whispers, animation and hope
rekindling, 'and I will leave her then. *Must* leave her

then. We could never stay *there*, the way she is now. No, we'll find a place of our own.' Then, overawed, almost incredulously, 'No stopping now,' and he draws one leg over both of mine, his genitals nestling in the soft hollow of my side, penis slowly stiffening and his face nuzzling into my neck, and we lie for a long while so, and I know that he is wanting me to roll over, but to do it in my own time, and I, too, am wanting that, his warm breath exciting me as it does, but a residual, solitary me that always saw fit to intrude if there was no other way, but resented the reverse of it, is listening to a lark singing somewhere high, is envying it its freedom and flight, is hesitating before a fusion that will forever change its shape as, just now, it had hesitated before diving from the weir.

At last, he lifts his head and, lingeringly and gently, takes my nipples in turn between his teeth, and at once my own erection begins and I lay a hand over my groin as though to hide a shame, but he as gently removes it, says, 'No! Face up to it, mate! All that time back there, you were lying to me and to yourself about what was going on, saying this, saying that, pretending that nothing had changed, but he,' and he flicks my penis into full erection with a finger and thumb, 'is telling you what you and me always knew.'

Then he brings his mouth to mine and forces his tongue between my teeth, and I am answering its grappling with an equal fury and starting, at last, to roll over, and he is sensing that and is readying himself, but I have delayed for too long. Laughing, exclaiming, crashing through the brush on either side of us, a party has come for a picnicking, is already riotously at the weir, and we scramble into our clothes, crouching low, and get our arses out of there, Danny muttering, 'Shit! *Shit!*' till we are out of earshot and he can howl it out to the not-listening sky.

We don't go back to the cottage, but to the bar, and sit there drinking beer and looking past each other till Danny hisses, 'Damn you! *Look* at me, Smith!' and I look at him and he says, more soberly, 'Are we going to start that all over again? This is not an ending, mate. This is a *beginning*. You just shake them up over there and get back quick as you can. OK?' and I say, 'OK,' and he fetches two more beers and touches his to mine and says, 'To us,' and I say, 'To us,' and we are almost forgetting I am going when the time comes to do just that and he has just thirty seconds to shake my hand – what else before all those seeing eyes? – and to ask, 'You still have your gun?' and I say, yes, but do I still need it *now*, and he says that one never knows, that life can deal a man bum cards when he least expects, but that's not the point, the point is that the guns are a *proof*, a proof that I can, anytime, anywhere, take into my hand and be glad.

Then the train begins to move and he reaches up to touch my hand again, his eyes at last harsh with tears, and I go on searching for his taut, motionless figure long after I can no longer see it in the gathering dusk, then slump into the nearest seat, turning my face to the face in the window beside me, watching it blur into the terrifying tremulousness of a drowning man's.

I touch the scar on my cheek and it flinches as though the long-dead tissue has a Lazarus-life of its own.

His letter beckons me. I take it up, scan it again. Phrases leap at me from its single page – 'When you read this, I will be meat ... gone, alone, to that other side of which we once spoke ... the quack says just a few more days ... The pain is *bad*, but not as bad as when I look back to how we were, how it could still have *been* ... or is it that I never *really* gave up, until now? ... Only time now for getting ready to go ... Anyway, I wouldn't *want* you to see the fuck-up I have become ... When I think of how I used to jog back there, how we wrestled and you never won –'

The second reading hits me as hard as the first. *Why* did I never go back? Haplessly, I search for a single clear-cut reason that will wrap it up, but it is not as simple as that, I entangled in the unpredictable thickets of my self. Images leap at me as did the phrases from that letter's searing page – pseudo-hero dying in a cardboard rubble on a makeshift stage, Douglas' face as I boot him up the arse, Douglas' cries as the Krauts carry him off, me, possessed, whispering 'Out, damned spot!', me balancing the scales, listening while a nightingale sings, waiting, like some damned tart, to be coaxed till the blood, too, sings – and there it stands – the bits-and-pieces, complex beast I must condemn.

Even then, I cannot do that without thrashing round. Was it only I that was flawed? Was there not also much that was questionable about *him*? Was there not, for example, something psychotic about the *intensity* of his friendship for me, his demands that it be anchored by pacts and vows? Was it not an almost impossible co-incidence that both of us should have been sodomized by our fathers when we were young? Did he not, per-haps, after hearing me cry out about that in my sleep, lie about his own father in order to foster a relationship that would culminate in the failed foreplay in the glade? Otherwise, why should he have been so willing to wear the dressing-gown of a man by whom he had been so cruelly abused?

I lay down the letter, stand at the window, stare out at the widening dawn, hearing only sparrows chirruping where nightingales have never been, and knowing with an at last wretched honesty that I don't believe any of these insinuations, will not be believing them even if they are true. Then I am looking down at the sleeping Carina, the pallid, formal doll that I decreasingly, duti-fully, seed, and I am wanting to be back in the bitter Eden, my hands beating on the postern of its skewed parameters, my heart calling out to the echoing empti-ness beyond.

Or is all this but a camp drama of my mind? His let-ter does not *berate* me! It is sad, but there is no calling me names. Does that not show that, at the end, there was an understanding and a forgiving and the postern is still a body's width wide? And the bequest which I have not yet unwrapped? Why should he have bequeathed me *anything* if the bond had not still been there? Fired by a new hope, eager to be absolved, I hasten back to the study, open the package with no longer hesitant hands, lay bare what it contains.

It is his gun.